TWILIGHT'S LAST GLEAMING

TWILIGHT'S LAST GLEAMING

American Hegemony and Dominance in the Modern World

Edmund Clingan

LEXINGTON BOOKS
Lanham • Boulder • New York • Toronto • Plymouth, UK

Published by Lexington Books
A wholly owned subsidiary of The Rowman & Littlefield Publishing Group, Inc.
4501 Forbes Boulevard, Suite 200, Lanham, Maryland 20706
www.rowman.com

10 Thornbury Road, Plymouth PL6 7PP, United Kingdom

British Library Cataloguing in Publication Information Available

Library of Congress Cataloging-in-Publication Data Available

ISBN 978-0-7391-7115-8 (cloth : alk. paper)—ISBN 978-0-7391-7116-5 (electronic)

∞™ The paper used in this publication meets the minimum requirements of American National Standard for Information Sciences—Permanence of Paper for Printed Library Materials, ANSI/NISO Z39.48-1992.

Printed in the United States of America

To my father, Eldon Clingan

Contents

Figures and Tables

Figures

Tables

Acknowledgments

I would like to thank Queensborough Community College of the City University of New York for granting me a Fellowship Leave for the 2010–2011 academic year, which enabled me to complete this project. College President Diane Call, Vice President Karen Steele, and the Lecture Committee invited me to give the annual QCC Presidential Lecture, which elicited some valuable comments on the topic of "Oil, Credit, and the Shifting Balance of Power."

The Columbia University Seminar on Law and Politics invited me to speak on some of the subject matter in chapter 4. Their questions and comments were very informative.

Professor Albert Berger of the University of North Dakota and Michael Wreszin, professor emeritus at Queens College, made suggestions at various points and provided encouragement and friendship.

Erin Walpole and Julie Kirsch at Lexington Books provided critical support. Joanne Foeller of Timely Publications copyedited the manuscript. My thanks also to the anonymous reviewer who pointed out weaknesses in the book and provided very useful comments for revision.

This book is dedicated to my father, who introduced me to the workings of markets and finance.

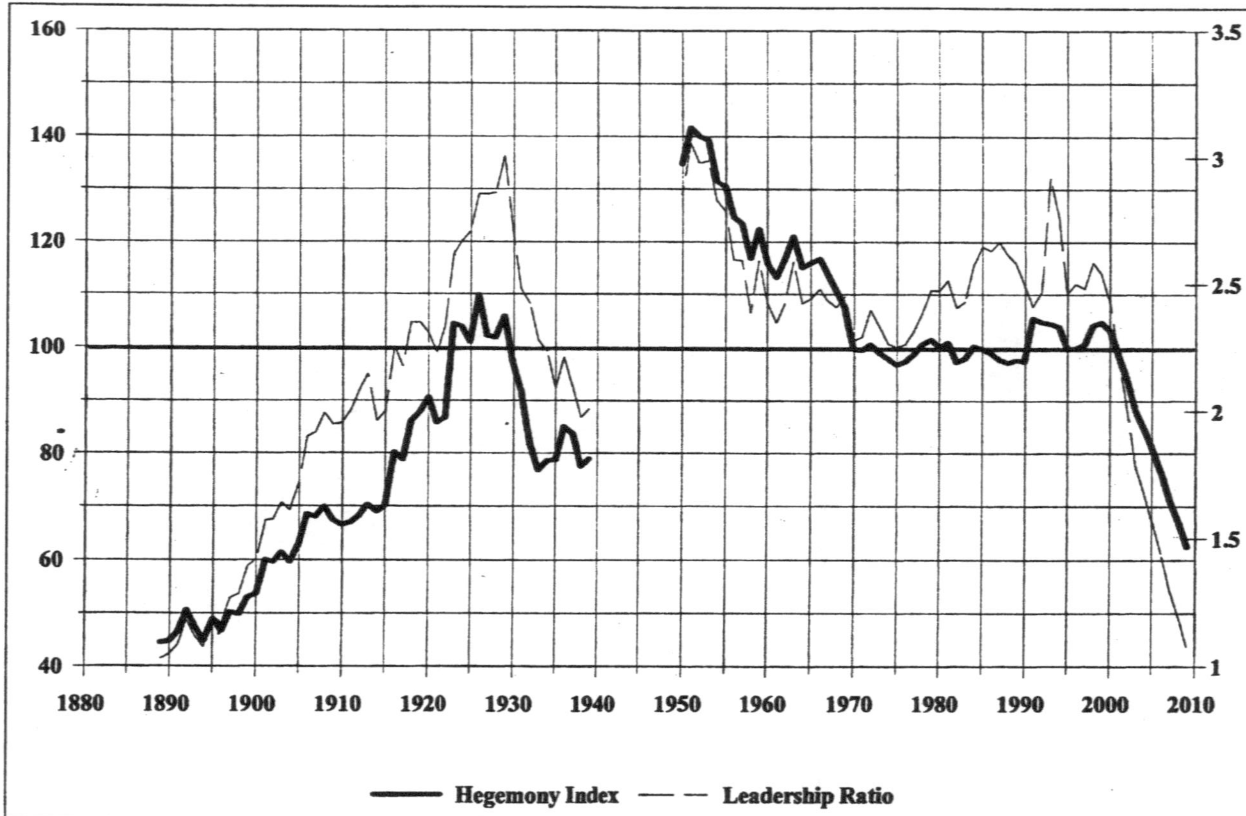

Figure 1.1 The Rise and Fall of American Dominance

1
Introduction

> With the Soviet threat now winding down, there is now a chance of concentrating resources upon America's own internal weaknesses, as both the revivalists and I propose. The difference between us is that I am somewhat more skeptical about the proposed reforms being implemented. In twenty years' time (which was what the final chapter of *The Rise and Fall of the Great Powers* was really all about), it will be interesting to see how much "revival" or "decline" has taken place.
>
> —Paul Kennedy, response to Joseph Nye, the *New York Review of Books*, October 11, 1990

We have passed the twentieth anniversary of Kennedy's reply and can make a judgment. While the United States did have a revival of economic and political influence, the decline since 2000 has left it in the weakest international position since before the First World War. This is not a subjective opinion but an objective fact backed up by statistics. The purpose of this study is to quantify the vague terms in international politics of "dominance" and "hegemony." It will illustrate the usefulness and limitations of these terms through the lens of the last two hundred years of international history. It will then focus on how the United States achieved first dominance and then hegemony. It will demonstrate how the United States lost hegemony and how it is now on the brink of losing dominance. Finally, it will suggest possibilities to regain dominance.

What Is Dominance?

Dominance in a power system indicates that a person, group, or country has the leading role in influencing other persons, groups, or countries. Dominance means that one is "first among equals" and that everyone uses the dominant as a standard. I agree with the Correlates of War project's definition of power as "the ability of a nation to exercise and resist influence."[1]

For the purposes of this study, dominance indicates the degree of difference between the leading and second-leading economies. The greater that difference, the greater the degree of dominance. Thus, according to the Conference Board Total Economy Database (TED), the United States in 2011, using EKS price-parity adjustments, had a GDP of $14.988 trillion while China, the second-largest economy, had an economy of $12.771 trillion. The American economy was 17 percent larger than the Chinese economy. We give it a dominance index of 1.17.[2] The dominant power will always have a number larger than 1; the closer a lagging nation is to a dominance number of 1, the closer it is to dominance.

What Is Hegemony?

Hegemony in a power system means an overwhelming dominance such that the country can regularly get its way.

For the purposes of this study, hegemony is achieved when the largest economy is far larger than the next biggest economy and is also larger than the next three combined. This indicates that even if an alliance could be built among the three next largest, it would not be enough to overcome the power of the hegemon.

Hegemony can bring political, economical, and cultural benefits. Others must use resources to meet a standard. The hegemon will be consulted on all major actions. While its veto power is not absolute, others will try to avoid offending the hegemon. Trade agreements will usually benefit the hegemon simply by creating a level playing field. Because much of the hegemon's power rests on its productivity, it can outcompete most others in most sectors as long as there are no grossly discriminatory barriers. The hegemon's culture also benefits. Its language is learned commonly and may even replace the native languages and cultures in other parts of the world. Others may copy its laws, customs, traditions, religion, inheritance practices, clothing fashion, music, and patterns of sex, marriage, and burial.

If the American economy of 2011 is compared to the three next largest (China, Japan, and India) it is 54.67 percent of those three; thus the hegemony index would be 54.67. Since this is under 100, the United States is clearly not close to a hegemonical position. This is a disconnection from the pronouncements of American politicians and media figures. In the past thirty years, the world has respected the United States as the dominant, not the hegemon. Even some American allies ignored its boycott of the 1980 Olympic Games. In the 1980s, Western Europe made financial and energy deals with the Soviet Union that were bitterly opposed by the Reagan administration. In 2003, the United States could not bully or persuade a majority of United Nations Security Council members to support the invasion of Iraq. Even Mexico, under a conservative government and in Washington's shadow, would not lend diplomatic support.

The Limits of Hegemony

Hegemony does not mean control. Never has even the strongest hegemon held total control or gotten everything it wanted. Ancient Rome was defeated in the Teutoberg Forest and could not extend its power to the Elbe River. China could not extend its power to Southeast Asia or nearby Japan.

Distance is a powerful limit on hegemony. With each mile, especially each mile from a sea coast, it becomes harder and harder to exert power. Unless one can bring overwhelming power to bear such as the Europeans on Africa in the late nineteenth century, or the Spanish on America in the sixteenth century, control on a large scale is impossible to maintain. The railroad and internal combustion engine temporarily eased these problems. Even in the cases of the Americas and Africa, the Europeans ultimately relinquished control. Modern technology makes it easier to communicate and transport goods and people across distances, but it also allows for more effective resistance.

The advent of mutually assured destruction has added another limit to hegemony. The overwhelming power of a hegemon can be balanced by the fear of damage from weapons of mass destruction. Even a relatively low level of damage can serve as a deterrent.

Modern nationalism has put another curb on the hegemon. Once upon a time, victory in war meant the addition of land with resources and a productive population. Now it means gaining control over a ruined land with a resentful populace. Winning brings few more benefits than losing. While cultural assimilation by the hegemon occurred regularly in the past, no measures short of genocide can bring a conquered area under full control.

The Debate over China's Gross Domestic Product and Per Capita GDP

The chief measure that I will use in this study is gross domestic product (GDP). This measures the output of a nation's population in a year.[3] It is useful for accounting both for the level of economic development as well as the size of the population. Different nations measure GDP in different ways, and there has been enormous debate over the question of purchasing parity. When there are restrictions on currency exchange and on prices, it becomes necessary to estimate the value of different economic goods and services. This book will rely on the studies done by Angus Maddison in a series of books for the Organization for Economic Cooperation and Development (OECD) and similar estimates as calculated by the Conference Board and the University of Groningen. These numbers (especially for India and China) have increasingly diverged from the estimates by others, notably the World Bank and the International Monetary Fund (IMF). If one accepted the latter's numbers, one would conclude that American hegemony still existed. Aside from the earlier examples, I think it is indisputable whether one looks at the gravity exerted by China on the world economy (especially on prices of raw materials such as oil), or military affairs, culture, and even sports, that American hegemony is long gone. In 2009, China's energy consumption surpassed that of the United States.[4]

The debate over the size of China reached a crisis point in 2006. Opinion divided sharply between two groups of scholars. The fundamental question was: did one believe (as did the CIA at the time and the OECD) that per capita GDP in China was about $6,800? Or was the number closer to $1,703, as the International Monetary Fund and the World Bank believed? This lower number was a straight conversion of the Chinese figures using yuan, even though the Chinese currency did not have full convertibility. The higher number already reflected adjustments based on the assumption that some reports were falsified. Maddison cut down the rate of growth from what is claimed by official Chinese sources by 10.6 percent.[5] At the time there were no middle numbers. I came to support the position of "rich China" in 2004, when China showed the ability to buy every drop of new oil that came on the market. Externalities could prove the case. Did China resemble one of the poorer nations or one of the middling nations? The World Bank and IMF in 2006 believed that per capita GDP in China ($1,703) resembled that of Angola ($1,873), Azerbaijan ($1,493), Cape Verde ($2,087), Egypt ($1,316), Georgia ($1,493), Guatemala ($1,995), Guyana ($1,729), Jordan ($2,219), Morocco ($1,725), Syria ($1,418), and Ukraine ($1,727). The OECD and the CIA stated that China's per capita GDP was $6,800, which put it in the company of Algeria ($7,200), Belarus ($6,900), Belize ($6,800), Colombia ($7,900), the Dominican Republic ($7,000), Gabon ($6,800), Lebanon ($6,200), Panama ($7,200), Peru ($5,900), Turkmenistan ($8,000), Ukraine ($7,200), and Venezuela ($6,100).[6] Oddly, Ukraine appeared on both lists, suggesting an equal problem measuring that economy.

Since the Conference Board took over sole responsibility for the TED, it has retroactively whittled its Chinese numbers as China's GDP steadily neared that of the United States. The 2010 TED indicated a 2006 per capita Chinese GDP of $6,374. This would be rather less in 2006 prices so they have trimmed about 7 percent, almost exactly the 2009 GDP gap. In 2007, the IMF and World Bank abandoned their ridiculous figures. Rather than accepting the artificial currency figures, they announced that they would accept a purchasing parity power that the World Bank's International Comparison Project had devised. They finally admitted that China was the world's second-largest economy.[7] Unfortunately, their PPP lowered the estimate that the CIA had accepted. The *CIA Factbook*, which had estimated the 2006 Chinese economy at $10 trillion, cut the 2007 estimate to $6.8 trillion.[8] The TED's downward revisions reached the breaking point with the 2010 release. It had extended its historical adjustment back to the 1970s to suggest that China's per capita GDP was lower than that of Cambodia. Cambodia of the 1970s sandwiched Pol Pot's genocide between two wars against the United States and Vietnam. It is highly unlikely that this beleaguered country was richer than China. With the 2011 release, the TED began to throw in the towel: by one price-parity adjustment (Geary-Khamis), China's economy was now larger. The gap between the two price-purchasing parity measures deviates by a whopping 29 percent. The Conference Board and the IMF seem to avoid the conclusion: China is about to become the world's premier economic power. The Conference Board's TED now ranks Chinese per capita GDP as being behind that of Azerbaijan, Turkey, Hungary, Costa Rica, and Croatia, and ahead of that of Mexico, Syria, Colombia, and Bosnia. The 2012 *CIA Factbook*, on the other hand, put China's per capita GDP behind that of Cuba, Thailand, Suriname, Tunisia, the Dominican Republic, and Jamaica, and ahead of that of Ecuador, Bosnia, Albania, El Salvador, Guyana, Turkmenistan, and Namibia.[9] Is China's wealth more likely to be among those in the first group or the second group? From that opinion hangs one's entire view of America's place in the world.

Are There Better Measurements?

GDP can be hard to measure. It is based on two even more difficult metrics. Each country has a foundation of assets including land, equipment, resources, labor force, and buildings. Labor produces goods from these assets. The greater the assets and productivity, the greater the GDP will be. Erosion of assets or productivity is bound to affect GDP sooner or later. Studies of American assets can range widely. The White House Office of Management and Budget published a 2004 figure of $52.4 trillion in total U.S. assets plus another $46.4 trillion in "education capital."[10] When one discusses productivity, one must decide whether to discuss the productivity of individual workers on the narrowest approach of an hourly basis (table 1.4) or the broadest approach of the entire population: men, women, and children, employed and unemployed. The broadest measure of that productivity would be *per capita GDP.* Let us set the cutoff of population at 3 million so as to eliminate small but oil-rich nations such as Equatorial Guinea and the United Arab Emirates. There is considerable difference among estimates because of disputes over currency conversions and purchasing parity. The CIA puts the United States in third place behind Norway and Singapore. The Conference Board agrees. But there is a problem. If we take the countries' own estimate of their GDP and population and simply use the current exchange rate, we get quite a different estimate. All of these currencies are freely convertible, so we do not have the same problem as we had with China's numbers. Norway is not so expensive that price parities can bring it down to the American level, so that suggests serious errors in PPP calculation. The United States does not crack the top ten with this measure and has less than half of the productivity of Norway. I will present all three estimates in index form in tables 1.1, 1.2, and 1.3. The point here is to show divergences in good-faith measures of wealth and productivity. All figures should be considered by the reader to be "in the ballpark," and one should focus on the trends, not temporary fluctuations. They all agree on this: the United States is neither the richest nor the most productive nation on earth.

So four different approaches to productivity yield quite different results. Many countries have fewer working hours than the United States. They prefer to "spend" their wealth in time off. In Norway, some workers have up to thirteen weeks off per year in paid vacation.[11]

The Relationship of Economic and Military Power

The importance of economic power to military success was aptly summed up by Mark Harrison in his introductory essay in *The Economics of World War II.* In the early part of that war, Germany and Japan were able to defeat an economically superior coalition. "The factors of strategic deception and surprise, speed of movement, skill in the concentration of resources and selection of objectives, martial tradition, and *esprit de corps* were all on their side."[12]

Harrison identifies *GDP* as important because it "sets an upper limit on military production." *Population* sets an upper limit for available soldiers. *Territorial expanse* helps determine the "quantity and diversity of natural resources" and the ability to form a self-sufficient economic block.[13] The

TABLE 1.1.
The Conference Board's Estimates of Per Capita GDP

Country, 2011	*Per capita GDP in 2011$ EKS PPP*	*Percentage of Singapore GDP per capita*
Singapore	$59,196	100.00%
Norway	$57,740	97.54%
United States	$48,087	81.23%
Australia	$47,149	79.65%
Switzerland	$46,882	79.20%
Austria	$44,681	75.48%
Netherlands	$43,879	74.12%
Sweden	$43,625	73.70%
Canada	$42,678	72.10%
Belgium	$41,179	69.56%
Germany	$39,301	66.39%
Denmark	$39,155	66.14%
Finland	$38,939	65.78%
Taiwan	$38,748	65.46%
United Kingdom	$38,184	64.50%
Ireland	$37,997	64.19%
Japan	$35,999	60.81%
France	$35,451	59.89%
New Zealand	$31,978	54.02%
South Korea	$31,745	53.63%
Italy	$31,741	53.62%
Spain	$31,211	52.72%
Israel	$31,167	52.65%

Source: The Conference Board Total Economy Database, January 2012, accessed May 30, 2012, www.conference-board.org/data/economydatabase.

fourth factor is *GDP per capita* because "the experience of two world wars has shown that, when poor countries were subjected to massive attack, regardless of size, their economies tended to disintegrate."[14] In World War I, Britain did far better than Germany or Russia because its per capita GDP was higher despite its small territory and a comparable economy. This allowed Britain "to supply its war effort with resources of superior quantity and quality, and at the same time maintained its civilian households in better shape from the point of view of personal health, living standards, and morale."[15] Table 1.5 takes Harrison's metrics on an evenly weighted basis to give us some idea of military potential. This does not state the balance of global military power, but gives one an idea of what that balance looks like

TABLE 1.2.
CIA Estimates of Per Capita GDP

Country, 2011 est.	*Per capita GDP*	*Percentage of Singapore GDP per capita*
Singapore	$59,900	100.00%
Norway	$53,300	88.98%
United States	$48,100	80.30%
Switzerland	$43,400	72.45%
Netherlands	$42,300	70.62%
Austria	$41,700	69.62%
Australia	$40,800	68.11%
Sweden	$40,600	67.78%
Canada	$40,300	67.28%
Denmark	$40,200	67.11%
Ireland	$39,500	65.94%
Finland	$38,300	63.94%
Germany	$37,900	63.27%
Taiwan	$37,900	63.27%
Belgium	$37,600	62.77%
United Kingdom	$35,900	59.93%
France	$35,000	58.43%
Japan	$34,300	57.26%
South Korea	$31,700	52.92%
Israel	$31,000	51.75%
Spain	$30,600	51.09%
New Zealand	$27,900	46.58%

Source: CIA, *The World Factbook, 2012.*

if each country completely mobilized its military potential. This is also a metric that one can use historically to examine power relations.

Flaws and Objections

GDP is imperfect, and so are most tools of economic and social measurement. The critic may object to overreliance on GDP and reliance on even hazier measurements of productivity and base assets. However, when one looks at the universe of international measurements, be they trade figures, balance of accounts, death rates, infant mortality, life expectancy, education tests, surveys on competitiveness, one finds that the GDP is the one statistic that is

TABLE 1.3.
Estimated Per Capita GDP Using Exchange Rates

Country, 2011	*Per capita GDP*	*Percentage of Norway GDP per capita*
Norway	$97,255	100.00%
Switzerland	$81,161	83.45%
Australia	$65,477	67.33%
Denmark	$59,928	61.62%
Sweden	$56,956	58.56%
Canada	$50,436	51.86%
Netherlands	$50,355	51.78%
Austria	$49,809	51.21%
Finland	$49,350	50.74%
Singapore	$49,271	50.66%
United States	$48,386	49.75%
Ireland	$47,512	48.85%
Belgium	$46,878	48.20%
Japan	$45,920	47.22%
Belgium	$45,712	47.00%
France	$44,008	45.25%
Germany	$43,742	44.98%
United Kingdom	$38,592	39.68%
New Zealand	$36,648	37.68%
Italy	$36,267	37.29%
Spain	$32,360	33.27%
Israel	$31,986	32.89%
South Korea	$22,778	23.42%
Taiwan	$20,101	20.67%

Source: IMF World Economic Outlook, April 2012, accessed May 30, 2012, www.imf.org/external/pubs/ft/weo/2012/04/data.

most kind to the United States and its role in the world. Thus the fundamental measurements that I use in discussing dominance and hegemony *are the ones most favorable to depicting American power.* If one chooses nearly any other metric, one may conclude as the French researcher Emmanuel Todd did: the empire is already over and the world is picking up the pieces.[16] This study is not quite so pessimistic.

The Correlates of War (COW) project, based at Penn State University, is a similar attempt to relate economic power to military power. This project has compiled a National Material Capabilities Set.[17] This moves more from

TABLE 1.4.
Output per Hour Worked, 2011

Country	*GDP per capita per hour worked in 2011$ EKS PPP*	*Percentage of Norway GDP per capita per hour worked*	*Annual hours worked per employee*
Norway	$72.87	100.00%	1423
United States	$62.14	85.28%	1705
Netherlands	$61.35	84.19%	1380
Belgium	$61.13	83.89%	1546
France	$59.67	81.89%	1441
Germany	$55.50	76.16%	1409
Ireland	$53.73	73.73%	1822
Austria	$53.52	73.45%	1663
Australia	$53.39	73.27%	1701
Sweden	$53.00	72.73%	1618
Denmark	$50.58	69.41%	1537
United Kingdom	$49.72	68.23%	1643
Finland	$49.19	67.50%	1698
Canada	$48.72	66.86%	1715
Switzerland	$47.11	64.65%	1628
Spain	$46.35	63.61%	1691
Italy	$44.27	60.75%	1770
Singapore	$43.49	59.68%	2287
Japan	$42.58	58.43%	1726
Taiwan	$38.67	53.07%	2174
Israel	$36.28	49.79%	1929
New Zealand	$36.15	49.61%	1704
South Korea	$29.03	39.84%	2204

Source: The Conference Board, Total Economy Database, January 2012, accessed May 20, 2012, www.conference-board.org/data/economydatabase.

potential to actual military power by basing its number on iron and steel production, energy consumption, population, urban population, military personnel, and military expenditures. It combines these into a Composite Index of National Capability (CINC). The database of Correlates of War goes back to 1816. It is an ambitious project, but this model can also lead in dubious directions. China's CINC in 1894 is at least five times that of Japan. I say "at least" because China's figures for military expenditure and urban population are unknown. China's big population and army dwarf those of Japan and overwhelm Japan's advantages. Of course, Japan easily won this war. Throughout history, small, well-trained armies have bested large, untrained

TABLE 1.5.
Index of Potential Equally Weighing Four Factors

2011	*GDP*	*Population*	*Expanse*	*GDP per capita*	*TOTAL*
United States	100.00	23.27	53.90	100.00	277.17
China	85.21	100.00	54.88	17.46	257.55
Russia	16.43	10.38	100.00	34.72	161.53
Canada	9.69	2.55	53.51	83.78	149.52
India	30.90	88.96	17.50	7.69	145.05
Australia	6.85	1.63	44.82	84.82	138.12
Japan	30.61	9.54	2.20	71.31	113.65
Germany	21.43	6.09	2.10	78.79	108.42
Brazil	13.58	15.22	49.76	24.12	102.68
United Kingdom	16.00	4.69	1.44	74.64	96.77
France	15.40	4.87	3.22	72.77	94.08

Note: To split the difference between the two measurement systems, this table bases the GDP index on the Conference Board figure and per capita GDP on the CIA figures. Population and expanse figures from *World Almanac 2012*, 732–34.

ones. This is where wealth comes in as a factor. COW says that urban population is a proxy for "higher education standards and life expectancies, with industrialization and industrial capacity." But it sets the urbanization level at 100,000 while admitting it is problematic.[18] It wanted to measure urban agglomerations after 1945, but the data were lacking.

The CINC figures also change radically when military potential is mobilized. Germany went from a CINC of 7 percent of world CINC in 1932 to 15.4 percent in 1938. British influence in 1816 is rated as the equivalent of the United States in 1947 (33.7 percent versus 31.7 percent of world CINC). Russia's CINC is absurdly ranked ahead of the United States' CINC from 1971 through 1988. I do not want to take away from this tremendously valuable database, I merely wish to demonstrate that no master number is perfect. With its emphasis on manufacturing power, it is no surprise that the COW shows that China's CINC passed that of the United States in 1996. In 2007, the United States had a CINC of 14.2 percent while China had 19.86 percent. By this measure and by TED's Geary-Khamis price-parity adjustment, China is already first among equals.

Historiographical Survey

This book draws much of its inspiration from Paul Kennedy's *The Rise and Fall of the Great Powers: Economic Change and Military Conflict from 1500 to*

2000. Published in 1987, it was not only a fine history of modern military and diplomatic relations, but tried to draw lessons and apply them to the present day. Kennedy was drawing on a tradition going back at least as far as the Prussian historian Leopold von Ranke.[19] Kennedy's thesis was stated simply:

> If . . . too large a proportion of the state's resources is diverted from wealth creation and allocated instead to military purposes, then that is likely to lead to a weakening of national power over the long term. In the same way, if a state overextends itself strategically—by, say, the conquest of extensive territories or the waging of costly wars—it runs the risk that the potential benefits from external expansion may be outweighed by the great expense of it all—a dilemma which becomes acute if the nation concerned has entered a period of relative economic decline.[20]

Kennedy was attacked as an economic determinist, despite his statement that "geography, military organization, national morale, the alliance system and many other factors" mattered as well. More serious scholars complained that for all his tables and charts, Kennedy did not try to quantify his argument. Many did not acknowledge that the revolutions of 1989 and the collapse of the Soviet Union in 1991 vindicated Kennedy. That the United States did not immediately break apart was taken as proof enough by some that Kennedy's reasoning was flawed and denied that "Great Powers in relative decline instinctively respond by spending more on 'security' and thereby divert potential resources from 'investment' and compound their long-term dilemma."[21]

At the time Kennedy published his book, he had to draw on early and halting studies of the history of global and national economic development. As one went back before the Second World War, estimates of national economies became more difficult and subject to wider errors. Trying to put them all on a level field with currencies and price inflation transformed the task from "difficult" to "almost hopeless." In the 1990s, Angus Maddison and the Organization for Economic Cooperation and Development published a series of revolutionary books. The first studies extended our usable data back to 1820. OECD then published Maddison's *Chinese Economic Development in the Long Run* in 1998. In 2001, OECD published an updated and expanded version entitled *The World Economy: A Millennial Perspective.* This has become the standard reference work for any serious scholar. That most information media and even some respectable institutions ignore it is scandalous. Maddison's data allow us to quantify with more precision than the scholars of the 1980s. Maddison's findings did not turn economic history upside down and largely confirmed the arguments that Kennedy was making.

Since 1991, books on international relations have fallen into two camps. There are "triumphalists" who proclaim that the United States is a hyper-power whose like has not been seen since the days of the Roman Empire. It can and should do whatever it pleases around the globe. Henry Nau stated in 2001 that Kennedy's predictions of American decline and the rise of the Pacific have not fared well.[22] When this group refers to international economics, it uses outdated and erroneous data. This approach became American government policy even as the economy cooled off from the prosperity of the 1990s. But a second group of writers said that even if intervention across the globe was moral and just, the United States did not have the military and economic power to carry it off. Andrew Bacevich in *American Empire: The Realities and Consequences of U.S. Diplomacy* summarized foreign policy under George H. W. Bush and Bill Clinton and tried to draw larger lessons. Under Clinton, the proportion of the American population participating in the military fell to its lowest level since 1940. He summarized the Bill Clinton/William Cohen policies of 1999 as "broad consensus on the inherent desirability of military power, a commitment to maintaining U.S. global military supremacy in perpetuity, support for maximizing the utility of the U.S. military might by pursuing ambitious activist agenda." Bacevich added a goal of maintaining order to aid globalization so the United States could reap rewards.[23] Charles Kupchan in *The End of the American Era: U.S. Foreign Policy and the Geopolitics of the Twenty-First Century* harkened back to the end of globalization that occurred in the 1920s and the Great Depression.[24] In Kupchan's view, even if globalization functioned properly, the market would inevitably create losers who would be discontented and work to undo globalism either within nations (inequality) or among nations. He saw the end of the American era stemming from growing isolationism and ignorance about the outside world. Domestic policy ruled international involvement. There were some gross generalizations about American regions and their relative hawkishness. Kupchan did not appreciate that the decline of the American economy since the 1950s in relative terms closed off the ability to influence many global events. An unwillingness to intervene was a reflection of an inability to intervene.

Kupchan credulously accepted the erroneous estimates of the Chinese economy provided by the IMF and the World Bank. They projected that China's exports would achieve second place by 2020 (it actually happened in the last half of 2006 and China became the leading exporter in 2010). There was also a complete dismissal of Russia, which has reemerged as a great power after a brief absence. Kupchan's critiques were valuable, but his thesis did not hold water in the end. The United States has contended with a multipolar world since the Vietnam War demonstrated the limits of the American economy and military. This was the end of the American era, though most Americans have been in denial ever since. The failure to repair the economy since Vietnam has been proved by the debacle in Iraq, a smaller, closer, and less jungle-bound nation. Chalmers Johnson's "empire trilogy": *Blowback*, *The Sorrows of Empire*, and *Nemesis* have also described aspects of international decline. No one would call these scholars radical thinkers.

Recent books have discussed the impact of China's rise on global relations. They run the gamut from denial to alarm to smug satisfaction. Robert Kagan, in *The World America Made*, denied any problem. Although he was aware of the Maddison numbers, he chose a comforting measurement from the U.S. Agriculture Department website, which claimed that the U.S. share of the global economy has not changed in forty years.[25] More alarmist was the book from former Dick Cheney aide Aaron Friedberg, *A Contest for Supremacy: China, America and the Struggle for Mastery in Asia.*[26] Friedberg believed that there will be stable and lasting peace only if China liberalizes politically.[27] Friedberg acknowledged the economic rise of China, as Kagan did not, and feared that the United States could lose "markets, technology, and vital resources."[28] Friedberg did not agree with right-wing hawks such as Jed Babbin and Edward Timperlake that China seeks war.[29] He believed that China is trying to prevent the United States from projecting air and sea power into the Western Pacific, to reduce its nuclear credibility, to deter potential nuclear attacks, and is starting to counter American naval supremacy.[30] The United States must mobilize resources to "stay in the game" and mobilize its allies to help.[31] While he called deliberate destabilization "inconceivable," he thought that only a weak and unstable China or a strong and democratic China would be accommodating.[32] His recommendations boiled down to a very large American military budget and "enhanced engagement" with more G-2 meetings, visits, and closer diplomatic and cultural relations.[33] Stefan Halper, author of *The Beijing Consensus*, denied that the United States and China can be partners in global management.[34] Halper suggested that China was knitting together a single Asian market "from Tokyo to Tehran" modeled on the Japanese empire of the 1930s.[35] While China would not bear the burden of leadership, it would promote a political and cultural agenda that challenged U.S. traditions. China set this ideological challenge of state capitalism against the failing "Washington Consensus" of the 1980s. It used its vast cash reserves, including $767 billion in U.S. treasury securities, to outbid others for vital resources such as oil.[36]

One can go too far in arguing for the ascendancy of China. Martin Jacques's *When China Rules the World* guessed that someday China will have a GDP four times the size of the American economy.[37] In 2010, the distinguished economic historian Robert Fogel estimated that by 2040, China's economy would be three times larger than that of the United States. I think both are wrong in this.[38] Jacques believed that the West was mistaken to assume that China posed primarily an economic challenge, that it would become Western (that is, embrace free markets, privatization, the rule of law, democracy, and human rights), and that it would accept the status quo.[39] While not as explicit as Halper, Jacques saw China reducing the rest of East Asia to the traditional tribute system of the Qing dynasty.[40] Only Japan is hostile to this plan, but in 2008, China passed the United States to become the leading importer of Japanese goods.[41] China provided loans to African nations with better terms and fewer conditions than the International Monetary Fund. There are also perhaps 500,000 Chinese expatriates in Africa.[42] It is close to becoming Latin America's leading trade partner.[43] Because of its history, China's "modernity characteristics" are different from those of the West, and it will approach global issues in a very different way.[44] While there is considerable overlap with Friedberg and Halper, Jacques did not see the setting of American dominance as an undesirable outcome. Bush's mismanagement and failure to guard American interests in Africa, East Asia, and Latin America opened the door for China.[45] A world of "many modernities" will not necessarily be a bad world.[46]

Having offered definitions of hegemony and dominance, this study will apply them to the early modern period and the nineteenth century. For centuries, China had what could be considered a hegemonic position over the world, but this did not lead to Chinese influence spreading. Chapter 1 will explain why. Changes of hegemony and even dominance are infrequent and some believe that they are always bloody. Nineteenth-century Europe saw two changes of dominance: Britain gained it in the 1820s and lost it by 1900. It is worth looking at this in greater depth because there is a dominance shift occurring now. Chapter 2 moves to the United States and how it rose to dominance and then hegemony. Building upon the British model of decline, it will show how and why the United States lost this hegemony from 1952 to 1973. Chapter 3 continues the story of the U.S. place in world relations after hegemony from 1973 to 2000. Chapter 4 then examines the specifics of how American dominance collapsed after October 2000 to the point where by one measure China stands poised to overtake the American economy and end 120 years of U.S. dominance. The financial meltdown of 2008 was not a bolt from the blue but the crescendo of a cacophony that had built since Election Day 2000. The conclusion considers the problems of post-dominance America.

Notes

1. Penn State University Correlates of War Project, National Material Capabilities Data Documentation, Version 4.0, NMC_Documentation.pdf, 1, last updated June 2010, accessed May 30, 2012.

2. These figures are in current dollars adjusted for EKS purchasing price parity. The Conference Board Total Economy Database, January 2012, accessed May 30, 2012, www.conference-board.org/data/economydatabase. Before 2007, the Conference Board shared responsibility with the University of Groningen and their numbers closely agreed with the figures of Angus Maddison and the Organization for Economic Development and Cooperation. If one uses the TED's Geary-Khamis price-parity adjustment instead of EKS, then China surpassed the United States in 2010 and has an economy that is at least 12 percent larger. I will discuss the divergences from the American Central Intelligence Agency and World Bank/International Monetary Fund numbers presently.

3. The TED defines GDP as "the aggregate measure of production equal to the sum of gross values added of all resident institutional units engaged in production."

4. Grant Smith and Christian Schmollinger, "China Passes U.S. as World's Biggest Energy Consumer, IEA Says," accessed May 30, 2012, www.bloomberg.com/news/2010-07-19.

5. Angus Maddison, *Chinese Economic Performance in the Long Run* (Paris: OECD, 1998), 153–54.

6. *World Almanac 2007* (New York, 2006) for CIA's numbers; IMF World Economic Outlook, January 2006, accessed May 30, 2012, www.imf.org/external/pubs/ft/weo/2006/01/data.

7. These revisions were marketed as cuts from a larger number that the World Bank had never promoted. Selim Elekdag and Subir Lall, "Global Growth Estimates Trimmed after PPP Revisions," posted January 8, 2008, accessed June 13, 2012, www.imf.org/external/pubs/ft/survey/so/2008/res018A.htm. "A Less Fiery Dragon? China May Be a Smaller Economic Giant Than Previously Thought," *Economist*, November 29, 2007.

8. *CIA Factbook 2008*.

9. TED January 2012; *CIA Factbook 2012*, accessed May 30, 2012, https://www.cia.gov/library/publications/the-world-factbook/index.html.

10. *New York Times*, December 5, 2005.

11. *New York Times*, July 25, 2004, quoting figures from the *Bergen Tidende*, suggested the Norwegian employees only work 195 days a year. This did not include time off for disability and long-term rehabilitation.

12. Mark Harrison, "The Economics of World War II: An Overview," in *The Economics of World War II: Six Great Powers in International Comparison*, ed. Mark Harrison (New York: Cambridge University Press, 1998), 1.

13. Harrison, "Economics of World War II," 2.

14. Harrison, "Economics of World War II," 18.

15. Mark Harrison, "The Soviet Union: The Defeated Victor" in Harrison, *The Economics of World War II*, 269–270.

16. Emmanuel Todd, *After the Empire: The Breakdown of the American Order* (New York: Columbia University Press, 2003), xviii–xxi.

17. Correlates of War, National Material Capabilities Set, posted June 30, 2010, accessed May 30, 2012, www.correlatesofwar.org. NMC_v4_0.csv.

18. Correlates of War, NMF_Documentation.pdf, 27.

19. Paul Kennedy, *The Rise and Fall of the Great Powers: Economic Change and Military Conflict from 1500 to 2000* (New York: Random House, 1987), xxiv.
20. Kennedy, *Rise and Fall*, xvi.
21. Kennedy, *Rise and Fall*, xxiii.
22. Henry R. Nau, "Why *The Rise and Fall of the Great Powers* Was Wrong," *Review of International Studies* 27 (2001): 579–92.
23. Andrew J. Bacevich, *American Empire: The Realities and Consequences of U.S. Diplomacy* (Cambridge, MA: Harvard University Press, 2002), 128.
24. Charles A. Kupchan, *The End of the American Era: U.S. Foreign Policy and the Geopolitics of the Twenty-First Century* (New York: Vintage, 2002).
25. Robert Kagan, *The World America Made* (New York: Knopf, 2012), 105.
26. Aaron L. Friedberg, *A Contest for Supremacy: China, America and the Struggle for Mastery in Asia* (New York: Norton, 2011).
27. Friedberg, *Contest for Supremacy*, 38.
28. Friedberg, *Contest for Supremacy*, 7.
29. Friedberg, *Contest for Supremacy*, 5.
30. Friedberg, *Contest for Supremacy*, 215.
31. Friedberg, *Contest for Supremacy*, 182.
32. Friedberg, *Contest for Supremacy*, 246, 252.
33. Friedberg, *Contest for Supremacy*, 255.
34. Stefan Halper, *The Beijing Consensus: How the Chinese Authoritarian Model Will Dominate the 21st Century* (New York: Basic Books, 2010), 217.
35. Halper, *Beijing Consensus*, 243–50.
36. Halper, *Beijing Consensus*, 23, 104.
37. Martin Jacques, *When China Rules the World: The End of the Western World and the Birth of a New Global Order* (New York: Penguin, 2009), 384.
38. Cited in Friedberg, *Contest for Supremacy*, 33.
39. Jacques, *When China Rules the World*, 8–12.
40. Jacques, *When China Rules the World*, 274.
41. Jacques, *When China Rules the World*, 311.
42. Jacques, *When China Rules the World*, 326–29.
43. Jacques, *When China Rules the World*, 321.
44. Jacques, *When China Rules the World*, 415.
45. Jacques, *When China Rules the World*, 313–21.
46. Jacques, *When China Rules the World*, 415.

2

Dominance and Hegemony in Modern Times

It is easy to consider the history of power in isolation and to quantify contemporary power relations. Combining history and quantification poses a severe challenge. In this chapter, I will present an "approximation" method to map out power relations when statistics are sketchy. This is subject to the same limitations laid out in the introduction. Next, we will consider power relations on the global and European scale in the nineteenth century leading up to the First World War. While the approximation and sketchy numbers suggest that China once held a hegemonic position, the text will explain why this was meaningless in a fragmented world. It will explain how and why the European powers overcame the seeming advantages held by China and India. It will then recast the international history of Europe using the new tools of this study and show why nineteenth-century Britain was a paper tiger and certainly not the hegemon that some claim. It will also explain how Britain lost even this weak dominance to Germany. The lessons of the falling powers China and Britain have considerable implications for today's world.

How Far Back Can We Take This Analysis?

We face several challenges in trying to set a baseline for our study. The time scale quickly exhausts much of our data. Economic numbers become more speculative before the twentieth century. Before the nineteenth century, they are largely guesswork. Censuses are less frequent and reliable. The productivity of the population can only be guessed at by extrapolating local or comparative studies. The precise value of assets destroyed by wars is unknowable. We are left with impressions: was the national population small, medium, large or very large? Did the people seem to be very poor, poor, well off, or rich? We can express this on a table, break it down into sixteen classes and plug in some contemporary examples (see table 2.1).

I used letters A thru P to give a rough sense of power relations, and I am slightly privileging wealth. The scale is 3.4 for each category. What would this table have looked like in 1960? Quite different. (See table 2.2.)

I have had to adjust the scale of per capita GDP to 2.6 because the gap between rich and poor has grown substantially. If I had used the same scale as in 2010, no nation would fall into the "very poor" category in 1960. What is striking about these charts from 1960 to 2010 is that most of the nations listed stayed at the same power level, despite moving from one box to another. Some grew in population, but became poorer. Some got richer but declined in population relative to other nations. In 1960, the United States was the only "A" country; today there are none. Both the United States and

TABLE 2.1.
Population and Per Capita GDP, 2010

PER CAPITA GDP	*Population (in millions)*			
	Small Under 32	Medium 32–115	Large 115–390	Very Large 390+
Very Poor under $1,450	P Malawi Sierra Leone Afghanistan Ghana	O Ethiopia Tanzania	M Nigeria Bangladesh Pakistan	J—None
Poor $1,450– $4,930	N Angola Iraq	L Egypt Morocco	I Indonesia	F India
Well Off $4,640– $16,762	K Albania Azerbaijan Belarus	H Argentina Iran Mexico Turkey	E Brazil Russia	C China
Rich $16,762+	G Norway Switzerland	D Britain France Canada	B USA Japan	A—None

Sources: IMF World Economic Outlook, April 2012. For India and China, The Conference Board Total Economy Database, January 2012.

TABLE 2.2.
1960 Population and Per Capita GDP (in 1990$)

		Population (in millions)			
		Small Under 10.4	Medium 10.44–41.75	Large 41.75–167	Very Large 167+
P *E* *R*	Very Poor under $565	P Mali Cape Verde	O Tanzania Burma	M Bangladesh (East Pakistan)	J—None
C *A* *P* *I*	Poor $565–$1,468	N Afghanistan Angola Ghana Sierra Leone	L Nigeria Egypt	I Pakistan Indonesia	F China India
T *A*	Well Off $1,468– $4,076	K Albania Iraq	H Turkey Mexico	E Brazil Japan	C USSR
G *D* *P*	Rich $4,077+	G Norway Switzerland	D Canada Argentina	B Britain France	A United States

Source: Angus Maddison, *The World Economy: A Millennial Perspective* (Paris: OECD, 2001).

the Soviet Union fell in the standings. China and Japan rose. Argentina and most of the big European countries fell. Note how Iraq went from "well off" in 1960 to "poor" in 2010 despite its oil riches. We will return to the cost of war and militarization. I suspect that there never has been a very large, very poor nation in history, though modern India seemed close at times. Malthusian restraints simply will not permit it. Either the nation will split apart with the richer areas taking care of themselves or there will be massive death from famine or government action.

What Did Dominance and Hegemony Mean for China?

There is always a dominant power, simply because one economy must be biggest. Hegemony is a rarer case. The first thing to discuss is global and regional hegemony. From the tenth to the fifteenth centuries, China almost certainly ranked as a hegemon on the global scale. It had the highest per capita GDP and the largest population of any political unit.[1] This "hegemonic status" was meaningless in practical terms. In a preindustrial and unglobalized society, there was no way to exert any kind of global dominance. Indeed China was dominated by the Mongol Empire for well over a hundred years. We may guess that the France of Philip the Fair was at a "D" or "C" level while China was at the "A" level, but that does not get us anywhere.[2] Although global links were forged starting in the fifteenth century, research by Jeffrey Williamson and Kevin O'Rourke indicates that a global economy did not rise until the 1820s. Their research focused on the price convergence of traded goods. Between 1820 and 1840, the link between rising crop prices and the rising cost of farmland was severed in Britain. This suggests that the global market now set the price of traded goods, not the domestic British market.[3] Similarly, O'Rourke and Ronald Findlay noted the convergence of prices for bulk goods.[4] Citing David Jacks, they confirmed that by 1835 there was an international wheat market.[5]

The long shadow of British textile manufacture fell across the plains of India in the 1830s and threw spinners and weavers out of work thousands of miles away. India before 1800 had made profits from its fine textiles. By 1825, it took 50,000 hours for Indian handspinners to produce 100 pounds of cotton, while the English machines could do it in 135 hours.[6] British control over parts of India prevented Indian rulers from raising protective tariffs to balance their disadvantage in productivity. India's imports of European textiles had been negligible, but between 1814 and 1830, the number exploded from 1 million yards to 51 million yards and grew another twenty-fold from 1830 to 1870.[7] Indian exports to other markets also suffered. Indian cloth had equaled 29 percent of the cotton cloth sold in Africa by British merchants before 1830. It fell to a 7 percent share in the 1830s.[8] As the steamship, railroad, telegraph, and telephone linked the world, global dominance became important.[9]

In 1820, as the era of globalization dawned, China enjoyed dominance and hegemony. The third largest economy of the time was probably the Mughal Empire. This "empire" had for practical purposes become a number of smaller states. Maddison lists an estimate of 16.04 percent for the boundaries of present-day India plus Pakistan and Bangladesh. Dividing that figure by

TABLE 2.3.
Share of World Economy, 1820–1910

	China	*Japan*	*USA*	*UK*	*Russia*	*Germany*
1820	32.92%	9.63%	1.81%	5.22%	5.43%	—
1870	17.23%	2.31%	8.93%	9.10%	7.59%	6.49%
1880	15.39%	2.47%	12.52%	8.93%	7.11%	6.99%
1890	13.53%	2.68%	14.17%	9.46%	6.61%	7.91%
1900	11.12%	2.63%	15.81%	8.92%	7.78%	8.52%
1910	9.42%	2.58%	18.39%	7.89%	8.63%	8.72%

Source: Derived from Maddison, *World Economy*.

two probably puts us near the mark. The Mughal Empire, Japan, and France (the leading European economy in 1820) combined were probably about three-quarters the size of the Chinese economy. That would put China's hegemony index in 1820 at 133. If we substitute Russia for the dubious unity of the Mughals, the hegemony index for China would be 160. (See table 2.3.)

A Chinese pundit of 1820, had he been able to see these figures, would have taken great satisfaction. No country was close to China in economic size. Its share of the world economy was probably not much changed from 1750.[10] Being from the rich side of the chasm, our imaginary pundit would not have cared about the massive divide between rich and poor in China. He could have, no doubt, pointed to massive production statistics. It was militarily dominant. Japan, which had invaded China in the sixteenth century, now was isolationist. The European powers were confined to a few ports. For all this apparent strength China was about to suffer catastrophic decline. It would lose about half of its world influence from 1820 to 1870 and then half again from 1870 to 1920.

What happened? To begin with, some of this strength was illusory. A rough estimation of per capita GDP in 1820 (table 2.4) reveals a starkly different picture. This is a different assessment than the Bairoch figures used by Kennedy. Those numbers found that there was not much of a gap between European and Asian GDP manufacturing per capita before 1750.[11] The new figures emphasize that there was a large advantage in agricultural productivity before manufacturing was mechanized. Indeed, this growth of productivity in the late seventeenth and eighteenth centuries is often called an "agricultural revolution." In Britain farm labor productivity more than doubled from 1700 to 1870.[12] Indian agricultural productivity seems to have fallen in the eighteenth century.[13]

One of the main features of the global economy of the eighteenth century, as in previous eras, had been Europe's long-term trade deficit with Asia, particularly India and China. After 1700, Europe substituted for imports

TABLE 2.4.
Per Capita GDP, 1500–1820 (in 1990$)

	China	*Japan*	*USA*	*UK*	*Russia*	*"India"*
1500	600		400	762		550
1700	600		527	1,405		550
1820	600	669	1,257	*1,707	689	533

Source: Maddison, *World Economy*.
Notes: Amounts for 1500 and 1700 are highly speculative.
*Figure includes Ireland; without Ireland it would be 2,121.

and promoted its exports. In 1701, the English Calico Act came into effect and restricted the import of silk and cotton goods. The Parliament raised the tariffs on imported plain calicoes in 1701, 1704, and 1708. In 1712, it raised the excise on domestically printed calicoes. Following riots and attacks on women wearing calicoes, a law of 1721 barred the wearing of this apparel.[14] One French merchant urged payments to attack and strip women in the street of their calicoes or alternatively to attire prostitutes in calicoes.[15] Chinese porcelain had been another high-value export. With subsidies from the king of Saxony, Johann Friedrich Böttger invented the first European hardpaste porcelain in 1709. A porcelain manufactory opened in Dresden, then moved to Meissen to preserve secrecy.[17] This had a catastrophic effect on Asia: it had steadily matched the former trade surplus by population increase, so wealth did not grow on average. We have no solid figures, but we may presume that the trade surplus was the first advantage lost by India and China. With a huge gulf between rich and poor, neither area possessed the kind of domestic market one might anticipate from a large population.[18]

The loss of productivity dominance was more than two hundred years in the making. During the Middle Ages, the European culture was deeply shaped by national competition and chronic labor shortages that put a premium on finding more productive ways to use capital. These forces allowed Europe to venture out into the Atlantic and begin successful colonization after earlier attempts in North America and the Eastern Mediterranean had failed.[19] The Black Death of the fourteenth century may have had the side effect of reducing economic inequality and giving a critical mass enough disposable income to maintain a domestic market for manufactured goods. There was certainly more peasant economic equality in 1450 than in 1700.[20] While early modern Europe had a large gap between rich and poor, there was enough wealth spread around that a domestic market could develop that consumed products of the colonies such as sugar and imported goods such as Indian cotton textiles and Chinese silk, porcelain, and tea. The seventeenth century saw the marriage of science and technology and the rise of scientific method that blossomed in the Enlightenment of the eighteenth century. The agricultural revolution that began in Britain after 1700 and in France after 1770 owed much to ideas of scientific farming.

I would suggest that productivity is a stool resting on three legs: health, transportation, and education. We have scattered ancient and medieval records that hint at infant mortality and life expectancy at birth. The baseline for life expectancy seemed to be age twenty-four. However, in the period 1425–1541, English life expectancy showed a definite swing upward. This was perhaps mirrored by Swedish records. The French records are for the 1740s, a war-torn decade, which may distort things. The major Asian areas still had life expectancies at the baseline of twenty-four through 1929–1931 (China) and 1891–1911 (India).[21]

The European cultures had steadily upgraded their waterborne transport. Starting with Vasco da Gama in 1498, the Europeans rounded the Cape of Good Hope and traded in the Indian Ocean, while no Chinese ship rounded the cape the other way until 1851.[22] In the late 1700s, Western Europe began to tackle overland transport using canals, iron bridges, and horse-drawn railroads. After 1815 came macadamized roads and then steam-powered railroads after the development of more powerful and compact steam engines. The macadamized road from London to Manchester saved at least half the time.[23] The Suez Canal of 1869 cut 4,000 miles from the Asian route and allowed steamships to make the journey.[24] Radicals of the Enlightenment such as Jean-Jacques Rousseau had called for universal education. Prussia became the first great power of Europe to institute public education around 1810 and gradually the other countries followed. These changes foretold that the productivity gap that had opened in the eighteenth century between Europe and Asia would get wider in the nineteenth.

By contrast, China was largely rural with a population of somewhere between 300 million and 350 million; there was no proper census and some provinces reported precisely the same percentage increase each year. The main resource was land, carefully improved and dammed over years: China reclaimed 7 million acres of land in the eighteenth century. The history of Chinese agriculture was hyperintensive cultivation of 10 percent of the territory. By contrast, 26 percent of the land in today's European Union is arable. There were few draft animals, tools, or storage facilities. China had plenty of labor but relatively few resources. The regulation of grain prices made peasant profit difficult. Education was concentrated in a class that seldom came up against the problems of agriculture and commerce. There was little credit and a limited currency in copper coin and silver bullion. The early Ming dynasty had experimented in paper money in the early fifteenth century to finance the building of a new capital in Beijing, the repair of the Grand Canal, and explorations in the Indian Ocean. This had led to inflation and a backlash against easy credit. China regarded itself as relatively self-sufficient; it neither encouraged nor heavily taxed trade and forced foreign merchants to live in Canton (Gwangzhou) from 1760 to 1834. It walled up the Portuguese in Macao with only a small volume of trade. It levied an equal amount of tariff on exports as on imports. It had no legal safeguards of trade, no investment market, no joint-stock companies.[25] China had no major regional competition as long as Japan imposed isolation on itself. Korea and Vietnam were small and weak. China had no appreciable railroad mileage until 1892.[26] There was no institutionalized science and invention.

Scholars devised an inductive method in the eighteenth century but they used it only to analyze classics. Publishing depended on the emperor. The government heavily taxed new businesses and often set up monopolies. Merchant profit went into land and education. According to R. Bin Wong, credit remained underdeveloped as the government tended to run budget surpluses and put the surplus into pawnshops to earn interest.[27]

Another problem was China's decaying internal stability. From 1775 to 1799, Chief Minister Ho-shen plundered the empire for his own benefit and installed relatives and cronies across the land. Officials fabricated tax and production reports. Diplomatic contact between China and Europe was almost nil. Japan under the shogunate knew more about Europe than China did. Europe knew more about China than China knew about Europe. In the 1780s a Chinese attempt to expand into Vietnam and Burma was defeated. China launched other "police actions" to suppress the Gurkhas of Nepal, two rebellions in Szechuan, and a rebellion in Taiwan (1788–1789). The weakness and corruption of the military was shown by the White Lotus Rebellion, which lasted from 1796 until 1804. This uprising occurred in a rugged area of the Han and Yangtze rivers. It was essentially a peasant rebellion, but the army could not put it down. This shattered the myth of Manchu invincibility.

To sum up: although the Chinese economy held a hegemonic position, it had lost its leadership in productivity (that is, per capita GDP) between 1400 and 1700. This was due to European nationalist and capitalist organization. This lag had intensified with the impact of the Scientific Revolution in Europe and the beginnings of scientific farming from 1700 to 1820. Over the next forty years, the Chinese hegemony crumbled. Somewhere around 1855, China likely lost its hegemony; it lost its dominance in 1888.

Shifts in trade and the end of the Chinese trade surplus opened a revolutionary situation in Asia. The habit of smoking opium came to China in the seventeenth century. During the late eighteenth century, annual imports of opium averaged sixty-seven tons a year. From 1800 to 1821, this average rose to three hundred tons a year. The price fell: a "chest" cost 1,000 to 2,000 Mexican dollars on average before 1821 and 700 to 1,000 after 1821. In 1838 China imported up to 2,660 tons of opium.[28] Population pressure, lower living standards, increased corruption, and general demoralization spurred opium consumption. Between 1820 and 1950, China lost one-quarter of its per capita GDP. The Chinese government had banned opium smoking and sales in 1729 and banned imports in 1796, but corrupt officials kept allowing it in.[29] India was the main opium source, but the Europeans controlled the trade and reaped most of the profit. Inflation from the trade deficit worsened the Chinese tax situation since some taxes were levied in copper and silver.[30]

China had tried to confine trade to Canton but that system now fell apart. In 1839 the empire moved against opium. The trade had upset exchange ratio between silver bullion and the copper cash used in everyday transactions. The government detained 350 British merchants, stripped them of their opium, and destroyed the drug. While the gap between rich and poor countries was not as great as today, table 2.4 shows that the advanced countries of the west were two or three times wealthier than the leading Asian economies. As we saw from Harrison's comments in the introduction, this allowed the west to supply its military efforts with better resources in both quantity and quality. The British sent steamships with cannon and four thousand regulars and sepoys from India against antiquated junks with primitive cannon. The Chinese military was organized to deal with bandits or rebels; it had no large land or sea units trained together with sufficient striking power. Its military vessels were much smaller than trading junks. Although China's economy and population were much larger than Britain's, the low level of per capita GDP made it vulnerable to a coastal war of short duration. Wisely, the British never attempted to conquer the Chinese interior. The Japanese experience in World War II showed that this would have been folly.

The Chinese administration continued to deteriorate. In 1852, the Yellow River, untended, began a massive shift hundreds of miles to north. This was its first major shift since 1194. Secret societies organized and rebelled against the ruling Manchus (Qing). The Taiping Rebellion, a religious cult based on the Christian Bible, broke out in 1850. It moved north and captured Nanking (Nanjing) in 1853. Every province rebelled, but the bureaucracy remained loyal. The revolts killed millions and destroyed precious capital. In the ports, Europeans asserted power and demanded more concessions. Russia seized western Manchuria and founded Vladivostock in 1860. At this low point, a coup brought new rulers to China who reorganized the army and bought western arms and training. In 1864, the government retook Nanking.

The difficulty of invading a distant area remained. By 1800, Korea was virtually independent. The French in 1866 attacked Korea but were defeated. Although the Europeans had larger economies and higher levels of per capita GDP, distance made a difference. France invaded Mexico in the 1838–1839 "pastry war." It had some success but failed to recover millions of dollars in defaulted loans. In 1846, the United States, with a smaller economy and about the same per capita GDP as France, defeated Mexico overwhelmingly. The shorter supply lines were critical.

The destruction of assets in China from massive trade deficits, rebellion, and environmental mismanagement caused the Chinese position to plummet even as Europe and the United States began to industrialize. The situation became more perilous after 1880 as Japan and Russia began to industrialize. In 1888, China lost its position as the leading economy in the world to the United States.

India's Decline in the World Economy

From 1813 to 1833, cotton manufacture in Bengal collapsed, throwing millions of Indian men and women out of work. Britain had at one time imported cheap Indian cottons; after 1833, cheaper British cottons inundated India. Even as Britain grew in wealth at the end of the eighteenth century, India suffered a number of problems. David Clingingsmith and Jeffrey Williamson have explored the deindustrialization of India. Upon the death of the Mughal emperor Alamgir (or Aurangzeb) in 1707, the empire was exhausted by that ruler's endless wars. South India fell away by 1725. A Persian invasion of 1739 left the capital Delhi in ruins. Mughal unity was destroyed "by a combination of interregional religious wars, court incompetence, greedy factionalism, and traditional interventions in the northwest for plunder."[31] In 1788, Afghans sacked Delhi and further weakened the most important power in India. This turmoil led to lowered agricultural productivity as men and animals were pulled away from production and the successors to the Mughals raised taxes. The rising price of grain in turn necessitated a wage increase for Indian spinners and weavers, which made their products less competitive in the world market.[32]

Lord Charles Cornwallis, the losing general in the American Revolution, had much greater success in India. He arrived in 1786 and seven years later promulgated a new law code for the areas then under British domination, mainly Bengal. The Cornwallis Code of 1793 laid the foundation of British rule until 1947. It mandated a major shift in Bengal landowning policy because it set permanent land assessments at a high level, forcing many of the old elite to sell their land. The purchasers were those with ready cash and their absolute right to that property was guaranteed by British law alone. This soon created a ruling class loyal to British interests based in the banking centers of Calcutta. The merchant/financier/tax farming class had been falling into poverty because of the simultaneous declines of the three great Muslim empires: the Mughal, Safavid, and Ottoman.[33] Bengal had suffered a catastrophic famine in 1770 but rebounded with rapid population growth in the nineteenth century.[34] The Bengal land tax raised more revenue regularly than most of the native states and served as collateral for 10 percent ten-year loans taken from both Europeans and Indians in the Calcutta money market.[35] As confidence grew, this interest rate fell to 6 percent.[36] This in turn led to British expansion in southern India and up the Ganges River to Delhi under the governorship of Arthur Wellesley. No occupation can last without the cooperation of a significant part of the occupied population.

Table 2.5 shows that England started the century running a huge trade deficit with India, importing at least 6.8 times as much value of goods as it sold in India. This should be taken as a conservative estimate in favor of the British. Smuggling of Indian goods was big business and the trade deficit was even worse than these figures suggest. In any case, the ratio narrowed by 1750 to 1.88:1, then expanded again to 2.67:1. As the volume of total trade grew, by 1790, the ratio had narrowed to 1.55:1. According to the Bairoch figures quoted in Kennedy, China lost about 60 percent of its manufacturing on a per capita basis from 1750 to 1900 but India lost 86 percent of its per capita level of industrialization.[37] India's share of world manufacturing fell from 24.5 percent to 19.7 percent from 1750 to 1800, then from 17.6 percent to 2.5 percent from 1830 to 1880. One must conclude that the second shift was the result of Britain's tightening political control. Textile manufacturing was hurt further as export commodities (opium, sugar, raw silk, raw cotton) became more profitable and drew workers away from textiles.[38]

India, whether considered as a collective subcontinent or as the Mughal Empire and other states, had never been dominant or hegemonic. Nevertheless, it had likely been the third-largest economy in the world in the early modern era. Its decline, like China's, was primarily a result of internal problems that were worsened by European pressure in the nineteenth century.

Dominance and Hegemony in Nineteenth-Century Europe

It is worth taking a closer look at the shifting balance of power in Europe from 1815 to 1914. If "rising powers inevitably use their strength for political, cul-

TABLE 2.5.
British Trade with "East India"

	Imports	*Exports*	*Deficit as % of imports*
England, 1700/1701	775	114	85.29%
England, 1750/1751	1,101	585	46.87%
Britain, 1772/1773	2,203	824	62.60%
Britain, 1789/1790	3,256	2,096	35.63%

Source: Data from chart by Phyllis Deane and W. A. Cole, *British Economic Growth 1688–1959* (Cambridge: Cambridge University Press, 1962), as reprinted in Jacob M. Price, "The Imperial Economy" in Marshall, *The British Empire in the Eighteenth Century*, 101.
Note: Annual average in £1000s.

tural, and military ends" (in Martin Jacques's words), does the European experience doom China and the United States to war?[39] It is sometimes asserted that Britain was the supreme power in Europe, but the economic statistics tell a different story. Britain passed France after fighting the wars of the French Revolution and Napoleon. Britain and France were then allies in the Crimean War. Germany passed Britain and then they fought in the First World War. Russia passed Britain and they were allies in World War I and World War II. It seems equally possible that the United States and China could be allies or enemies in a war, based on the historical record.

In the aftermath of Napoleon's defeat, France remained the largest economy in Europe. Many political scientists describe a nineteenth-century British hegemony that simply did not exist.[40] Britain came out of the Napoleonic Wars with a national debt more than twice its GDP. This debt was not reduced under 100 percent of GDP until after 1860.[41] Somewhere in the 1820s, probably, the United Kingdom passed France and reached the height of its power in Europe around 1890. Bairoch puts the shift between Britain and France in the latter 1830s.[42] Even then however, its hegemony index was only 45.8 compared to the next three leading economies. Britain's money remained shaky: it had suspended gold convertibility in 1797, then restored it in 1819. However, bubbles in insurance and foreign bonds led to a hemorrhage of gold and the Bank of England had to beg for a humiliating bailout by France to the tune of £400 million in 1825.[44] France had been losing ground to Britain for the better part of a century. Its agriculture lagged by at least seventy years. At a time when horsepower was measured by real horses, France had a large energy deficit. By the 1820s, Britain had used a number of advantages

TABLE 2.6.
Share of World Economy: European Powers, 1820–1910

	UK	*Russia*	*Germany*	*France*	*Austria (exc. Italy)*	*Italy*	*Hegemony*
1820	5.22%	5.43%		5.53%	2.12%		41.579 (French)
1870	9.10%	7.59%	6.49%	6.55%	2.65%	3.80%	44.111
1880	8.93%	7.11%	7.63%	5.67%	2.82%	3.55%	43.753
1890	9.46%	6.61%	8.62%	5.42%	2.97%	3.41%	45.811
1900	8.92%	7.78%	9.28%	4.99%	2.83%	2.97%	42.785
1910	7.89%	8.63%	9.65%	3.96%	2.78%	3.33%	47.10 (German)

Source: Derived from Maddison, *World Economy*.
Note: Part of the shift between France and Germany from 1870 to 1880 was the latter's acquisition of Alsace-Lorraine from the former.

to launch industrialization and overtake France. Britain showed growing financial sophistication with open-market operations and limited liability. This sophistication averted a repeat of the 1825 bailout and harnessed British wealth to the cause of economic development.

This account updates and subtly recasts the figures Kennedy used in 1987. Those numbers stressed the size of the Russian economy, and saw only Britain having a larger economy in the 1850s. Bairoch and Kennedy suggested that total product was of little import because in an agricultural society, most of the product is immediately consumed. "It is far less likely to lead to surplus wealth or military striking power." One of the keys to the rise of British power was the low percentage dedicated to the military. Kennedy estimated that from 1815 to 1870, the British spent only about 2 to 3 percent of its GNP on the military. This freed up capital for investment. In keeping with Harrison's remarks on per capita GDP, let us note that France and Britain, having only a slightly larger military combined than Russia, were able to travel to the Crimea and defeat Russia in the war of 1854–1856. The Correlates of War project gives Britain and France a combined CINC of .418 versus .135 for Russia. While it may be true that the British economy was "less 'mobilized' for conflict than at any time since the early Stuarts," Britain had a strong enough military to fulfill its needs.[45] Had the British poured in money to attempt a large-scale venture such as the conquest of China or the breaking of Russian power, they would have failed and destroyed their economy. Bairoch underestimates the effect of total volume of GDP. As wars drag on, the overall volume becomes more significant and the per capita GDP less significant. In the eighteenth-century imperial conflicts between Britain and France, one sees the same pattern: the French military did very poorly in the first years of the war, then began to recover as splits developed in Britain. Britain quickly wrapped up a peace treaty with surprisingly modest gains considering the apparent course of battle: this is seen in the Utrecht treaty of 1713, Aix-la-Chappelle 1748, and the Paris treaty of 1763. We do not have anything like adequate economic numbers, but it seems clear that by the time of Napoleon, the French gained a dominance in Europe that could only be overthrown by the combined efforts of the other four great powers. The French Empire that included the Low Countries, the Rhineland, and northern Italy may have been very close to a European hegemon. Britain demonstrated enormous national willpower in defeating Napoleon. The percentage of debt accumulated by Britain is generally only seen in losing nations before economic collapse. Kennedy is wrong to describe mid-nineteenth-century France as a "middle power." It was a front-rank power until it lost Alsace-Lorraine, and it is instructive to note that today no part of France seems in danger of slipping away as Ireland, Silesia, Ukraine, and other "inalienable" parts of empires have been lost over the years. These revised economic numbers more closely mirror the actual economic and diplomatic events of nineteenth-century Europe than the older estimates. After 1815, Britain did not have the financial resources for major commitments nor would national will have supported a prolonged war in China or Russia. The Franco-Prussian War marked a major turn. Before it, France and "Germany" were fairly evenly matched. The shift gave the Germans a leading position. Around 1895, Britain lost its dominant position to Germany. On the eve of World War I, Germany was more dominant than Britain had ever been.

Britain's Loss of Dominance

From 1890 to 1910, Britain lost about one-sixth of its world economic share. This is not as dramatic a decline as China's, but Britain did not start out with a hegemonic position, and its loss of dominance had a large impact. The reasons for the decline of Britain have been disputed. Table 2.6 shows that the balance had been shifting since 1870 when Britain's dominance over the second-leading nation (France) was probably at its apogee. From 1890 to 1910, Germany and Russia overtook Britain. We should first qualify this by looking at the shift in GDP per capita to factor out pure population growth. We will put the British per capita GDP (including Ireland) in 1913 as the base and compare it to Germany and Russia. These are more comforting numbers for Britain because it shows that some of the growth of the German and Russian economies was due simply to faster population growth, although the Germans were closing the gap in terms of productivity and wealth. To begin with, there was a loss of population in the United Kingdom. Almost half of the European migrants from 1870 to 1913 came from the United Kingdom, 6.4 million persons.[46] Had all these people stayed and generated an average

TABLE 2.7.
Per Capita GDP Index, 1890–1913

	Britain	*Germany*	*Russia*	*British advantage over Germany*
1890	81.5	51.6	18.8	1.579
1900	91.4	63.7	24.8	1.435
1910	93.8	71.7		1.308
1913	100.0	78.3	30.2	1.277

Source: Maddison, *World Economy*.
Note: Britain 1913 = 100.

per capita GDP, Britain's overall GDP would have been essentially the same as Germany's. One problem was the collapse of the British agrarian sector due to free trade and foreign competition. Much of this migration (and not just Irish) came from the countryside.[47]

Kennedy cites two long-term problems for Britain's loss of dominance. The first was its willingness to invest in other nations that had greater resources and just needed to take off, such as the United States. The second was an overdependence on international trade and especially international finance. I think these mask deeper problems. The first suggests a lack of opportunity in domestic investment; however, international investment benefits everyone in most cases. The second only becomes an issue in case of major war, and the point of power is to make sure that a war never comes.

The first deep problem of Great Britain was careless diplomacy after 1865. Between 1815 and 1853, the British concentrated on diplomacy and saved the military aspect for a quick decisive strike, often a naval strike after it had set up the circumstances. Diplomacy and threats secured Latin American independence and new markets for British goods. It sank the Turkish-Egyptian fleet at Navarino without causing an extended war. Diplomacy in 1833 allowed a concession to Muhammad Ali Pasha of Egypt. A brief landing of British force in Beirut and Acre in October/November 1840 forced the Egyptians back with minimal strife. It is probably appropriate to call this "Palmerstonian foreign policy" since Lord Palmerston was war secretary from 1807 to 1828 and foreign secretary from 1830 to 1841 and 1846 to 1851. He served as prime minister from 1855 to his 1865 death with only one short interruption. Palmerston's motto was "Britain has no eternal allies and no perpetual enemies, only interests that are eternal and perpetual."[48] Palmerston's big misstep was the Crimean War, although he was occupying the Home Office at the time of its start and is perhaps partly innocent. At the end of his life, Palmerston tried to aid the Danes, who had broken a treaty signed in London but were being thrashed by the Prussians and Austrians. Palmerston seemed to realize that the rise of a united Germany would change the balance of power. After his death, Britain allowed German unification and spent the latter half of the century in isolation.

This foreign policy after 1865 included a thoughtless move to an expensive empire. The territories acquired between 1865 and 1900 were mostly economically unproductive and even running an empire on the cheap, they cost the British money. These territories did not duplicate the Indian example of providing a market for British manufactures. In 1913, the British colonies (excluding the Dominions and India) accounted for only 6.3 percent of British exports and 3.9 percent of British investment. Britain ran a trade deficit with them equal to 15 percent of imports. In 1934, these colonies accounted for 10.8 percent of exports, 6.2 percent of investment, and the trade deficit equaled 29 percent of imports from these colonies.[50] Herbert Frankel estimated that £941,307,000 were invested in British Africa between 1870 and 1936.[51] The Boer War alone cost £230 million.[52] On the continent, even socialists were caught up by colonial fever. Had the money and effort been directed to productive purposes, Britain might have retained its dominance. Imagine the impact of the money wasted in the Boer War had it been used to modernize the British industrial and educational system. A globe of 1914 painted with so much British color may look impressive, but even if we added the economies of all the colonies and dominions, it would not have given the British hegemony.

The second deep problem was the failure to invest in education. British per capita GDP was roughly twenty years ahead of France's. It may be that the crushing debt from the Napoleonic Wars prevented the British from investing in primary education in anticipation of France's laws of 1833 (the Guizot Law) and 1850 (the Falloux Law). The French completed the system with the Ferry Laws of the early 1880s. By 1869, when the debt was finally below 100 percent of GDP, Britain should have had compulsory elementary and secondary education and a beefed-up university system. In fact, it had none of these. The British Central Society of Education, which called for state education, was only founded in 1836 and was considered radical. In 1839, the Whig government of Lord Melbourne introduced a modest plan to create secular teachers' colleges, increase by 50 percent the tiny grants to the Anglican and Dissenting churches that supervised education, and give grants according to needs. This modest bill failed.[53] Amazingly in 1840, half or more of the men living in eight of the forty-four counties of England and Wales could not sign their names in the marriage register.[54] In 1843, the Conservative government of Sir Robert Peel and Sir James Graham proposed a bill to create state schools for children of the poor and factory workers. This bill also failed.[55]

Theo Hoppen notes that German schooling exceeded British education with 97.5 percent of children between ages six and fourteen attending school in 1860.[56] In 1851, 41 percent of British children aged ten to fourteen were in school; that rose to 53 percent by 1871.[57] Unfortunately, Hoppen then equates "education" with "science" and demonstrates the funds spent on British science were comparable and that Rugby, Harrow, Winchester, Clifton, and the major universities put a new emphasis on science.[58] This is a common error. Since the Sputnik scare of 1957, the United States has periodically boosted science and math education. This has only had the effect of depriving Americans of the rounded base they need to appreciate science and creating a generation of science teachers unable to teach effectively. The result can be seen in college departments of science and engineering and just about any international yardstick: the United States has ceded its technical leadership and depends on men and women born elsewhere. *Overall* education is the key. A scientist unable to write effectively is useless. In 1870, the Liberal Gladstone government introduced a bill to provide education through Board Schools for most children; this bill gained momentum and became law after the smashing Prussian military victories over France in the summer of 1870.[59] Education became compulsory in 1880, and by 1885, British spending on education was probably close to the spending on the Royal Navy.[60] In 1891, the Salisbury government made elementary education free.[61] At Oxford and Cambridge, non-Anglican students were barred until the 1850s.[62] The 1899 Education Act extended compulsory schooling to age twelve, but secondary education lay beyond lower-class children until the 1902 Education Act.[63] J. M. Roberts quotes the estimate that only 0.5 percent of British children reached secondary education in 1896.[64] The Act of 1902 would create "by 1914, over 1,000 secondary schools, . . . 349 of them for girls."[65] By 1914, Great Britain, the richest nation in Europe, had caught up to where Prussia was in 1860. Germany's production of graduate engineers towered over England's.[66] Germany's superior instruction system allowed it to vault over England in the chemicals sector during the 1880s.[67] Germany also became the European leader in electricity production. British university education lagged. In 1881, the university student population in England was 10,560; ten years later, it was about 16,000.[68] In 1914, it was 18,228, while Germany had 60,000.[69] England's ratio of university students to total population was lower than that of Scotland or Ireland.[70]

The third deep problem concerned trade. Free trade itself did not cause problems, but other problems were exacerbated by free trade. When Britain abandoned free trade in the early 1930s, it did no good. Britain began to run a trade deficit in 1907. This trend had developed gradually. In the late 1860s, the United Kingdom produced three-quarters of the food and wool it consumed. In ten years, this was down to half.[71] By the 1880s, it was dangerously dependent on trade to supply three-quarters of grain and 40 percent of its meat. From 1875 to 1885, the land area of wheat farming had shrunk by 30 percent. The wheat crop fell 6 percent from 1897 to 1912. In 1912, Great Britain spent £260 million on imported food, £100 million more than Germany did.[72] By 1914, it had to import 80 percent of its grain.[73]

By the 1880s, alarm was growing at possible disruption of food supplies. The government would neither subsidize agriculture nor would it consider trade barriers since trade made up a disproportionate share of the British economy. Britain failed to invest in its agriculture or move into commercial agriculture as Denmark did in this time. It resorted to building up the Royal Navy. The military budget in 1887 was £30 million (2.1 percent of GNP). By

1898, it reached £47 million (2.56 percent of GNP). All this did was spark an arms race. As G. R. Searle points out, when the race began in 1883, Britain's capital ships equaled those of Russia, France, the United States, Japan, Italy, and Germany combined. By 1897, the British capital fleet only amounted to about two-thirds of the other nations' fleet. Germany was just beginning to build a major navy.

The Boer War demonstrated that Britain was in difficult straits. Since the Crimean War, it had eschewed any formal alliances. In 1899, it went to war against the small southern African republics. The Boers were better armed and initially outnumbered the British forces. The British resorted to brutal tactics and set up concentration camps in southern Africa and in colonies such as St. Helena and Ceylon.[74] Twenty-eight thousand Boers, mostly women and children, died.[75] When the Boers surrendered in 1902, the cost to the British was great: about 22,000 dead, over 110,000 wounded, and a price over one-quarter of the cost of the war against the French Revolution and Napoleon.[76] The four years of war were funded by borrowing: the budget deficit in 1900 reached £53.2 million (2.59 percent of GNP), the worst since 1815.[77] In 1903, the national debt hit £798.3 million, which was 37.85 percent of GNP. In Britain, taxes had declined steadily since 1816 when they were perhaps one-quarter of the GNP. In 1853, the revenues as percentage of GNP was 9.25 percent. In 1902, it was 7.63 percent. The government raised revenue rates to 8.49 percent by 1910 to pay for debt, military spending, and social insurance programs.[78]

While Germany was no pacifist state, it reserved enough resources to develop into the leading economy of Europe. Its base was an educational system that gradually encompassed more students during the course of the nineteenth century. It succeeded in training scientists, engineers, and skilled workmen. Germany took the lead in emerging sectors such as chemicals and electrical equipment. It kept pace in building railroads that complemented its river system. Germany pioneered social insurance programs and had far less colonial exposure than Britain or France.

After 1900, having lost dominance, successive British governments began to take decisive steps. The Conservative Salisbury and Balfour governments came to understandings with Japan and the United States and signed the Entente Cordiale with France. They reluctantly passed secondary education bills. The Liberal Campbell-Bannerman and Asquith governments reached a colonial settlement with Russia and erected health and old age protections in imitation of Germany. Given time, improved education and health programs might have restored Britain to a dominant position. That hope vanished in the cataclysm of the First World War, and when the smoke cleared the United States had entered its first era of hegemony.

Before the twentieth century, dominance and hegemony had played a limited role in world affairs. China came into the century enjoying dominance and hegemony on paper, but its low productivity and poverty made China vulnerable to short wars along its exposed coastline. Assets gushed out of China at an accelerating rate until the political and economic systems stood on the brink of the abyss. Within Europe, industrializing Britain held a position of dominance from the 1820s until 1900. The immense debt remaining from the Napoleonic Wars hamstrung Britain for much of this time. Britain stayed out of subduing the continent and relied on diplomatic skills and short military actions. After 1865, Britain paid a price for misallocating resources to colonial conquest and arms races. It failed to keep up on education and fell behind Germany and Russia. The attempts to remedy these mistakes after 1900 came too little, too late. Though the nineteenth century was born and died in blood, it is too simple to attribute this to the shift of power to and away from Britain. Firstly, Britain never had much of an advantage and was never a hegemon. Secondly, the timing does not match. Thirdly, Britain allied with its putative rivals as often as it warred with them. This bodes well for a twenty-first century of cooperation, not battle.

Notes

1. Angus Maddison, *Chinese Economic Performance in the Long Run* (Paris: OECD, 1998), 13.
2. Maddison, *Chinese Economic Performance*, 20.
3. Kevin O'Rourke and Jeffrey G. Williamson, "When Did Globalization Begin?" *European Review of Economic History* 6 (2002): 23–50.
4. Ronald Findlay and Kevin O'Rourke, *Power and Plenty: Trade, War, and the World Economy in the Second Millennium* (Princeton, NJ: Princeton University Press, 2007), xxiv.
5. Findlay and O'Rourke, *Power and Plenty*, 404.
6. Findlay and O'Rourke, *Power and Plenty*, 320.
7. Paul Kennedy, *The Rise and Fall of the Great Powers: Economic Change and Military Conflict from 1500 to 2000* (New York: Random House, 1987), 148.
8. Findlay and O'Rourke, *Power and Plenty*, 413.
9. Tirthanker Roy, "Economic History and Modern India: Refining the Link," *Journal of Economic Perspectives* 16:109–30.
10. Paul Bairoch suggested that the Chinese share of world manufacturing was 32.8 percent in 1750, 29.8 percent in 1800, and 29.8 percent in 1830. "International Industrialization Levels from 1750 to 1980," *Journal of European Economic History*, Fall 1982, 296–304.
11. Kennedy, *Rise and Fall*, 148.

12. Farm production grew by 181 percent while the farming workforce grew slightly. Rondo Cameron, *A Concise Economic History of the World: From Paleolithic Times to the Present,* 2nd ed. (New York: Oxford University Press, 1992), 168.

13. David Clingingsmith and Jeffrey G. Williamson, "Deindustrialization in 18th and 19th Century India: Mughal Decline, Climate Shocks and British Industrial Ascent," *Explorations in Economic History* 45, no. 3 (2008): 218.

14. Julian Hoppit, *A Land of Liberty? England 1689–1727* (New York: Oxford University Press, 2000), 275.

15. Fernand Braudel, *Civilization and Capitalism 15th–18th Century,* vol. 2, *The Wheels of Commerce* (New York: Harper and Row, 1982), 178.

16. Ulrich Pietsch, "The Royal Porcelain Collection," *The Glory of Baroque Dresden: The State Art Collections Dresden* (Jackson, MS: Mississippi Commission for International Cultural Exchange, 2004), 179.

17. R. R. Palmer and Joel Colton, *A History of the Modern World,* 7th ed. (New York: McGraw-Hill, 1992), 259.

18. Alfred W. Crosby, *Ecological Imperialism: The Biological Expansion of Europe, 900–1900* (New York: Cambridge University Press, 1986), 42–69.

19. George Huppert, *After the Black Death: A Social History of Early Modern Europe,* 2nd ed. (Bloomington, IN: Indiana University Press, 1998), 74.

20. Angus Maddison, *The World Economy: A Millennial Perspective* (Paris: OECD), 29–30.

21. David Landes, *The Wealth and Poverty of Nations: Why Some Are So Rich and Some So Poor* (New York: Norton, 1998), 96.

22. Findlay and O'Rourke, *Power and Plenty,* 376.

23. Findlay and O'Rourke, *Power and Plenty,* 380.

24. John King Fairbank et al., *East Asia: Tradition and Transformation,* rev. ed. (New York: Houghton Mifflin, 1989), 437–40.

25. Brian Mitchell, *International Historical Statistics: Africa, Asia, and Oceania* (New York: Stockton Press, 1995), 667.

26. R. Bin Wong, *China Transformed: Historical Change and the Limits of European Expansion* (Ithaca, NY: Cornell University Press, 1997), 133.

27. Fairbank et al., *East Asia,* 450–51.

28. Fairbank et al., *East Asia,* 452.

29. Wong, *China Transformed,* 238.

30. Fairbank et al., *East Asia,* 612.

31. Stanley Wolpert, *A New History of India,* 2nd ed. (New York: Oxford University Press, 1982), 168–73.

32. Clingingsmith and Williamson, "Deindustrialization," 215–23.

33. Rajat Kanat Ray, "Indian Society and the Establishment of British Supremacy, 1765–1818," in *The Oxford History of the British Empire: the Eighteenth Century,* ed. P. J. Marshall (New York: Oxford University Press, 1998), 515.

34. Ray, "Indian Society," 514.

35. Ray, "Indian Society," 517–18.

36. Ray, "Indian Society," 522.

37. Kennedy, *Rise and Fall,* 149.

38. Clingingsmith and Williamson, "Deindustrialization," 216.

39. Martin Jacques, *When China Rules the World: The End of the Western World and the Birth of a New Global Order* (New York: Penguin, 2009), 12.

40. Charles Kupchan, *The End of the American Era: U.S. Foreign Policy and the Geopolitics of the Twenty-First Century* (New York: Vintage, 2002), 74; Robert Kagan, *The World America Made* (New York: Knopf, 2012), 43; Aaron L. Friedberg, *A Contest for Supremacy: China, America and the Struggle for Mastery in Asia* (New York: Norton, 2011), 4.

41. Compare British debt figures from Charles P. Kindleberger, *A Financial History of Western Europe*, 2nd ed. (Oxford: Oxford University Press, 1993), 162, table 9.1, with economic figures from Mitchell, *European Historical Statistics*, abridged ed. (New York: Columbia University Press, 1978), 408, and Angus Maddison, *The World Economy: A Millennial Perspective* (Paris: OECD, 2001).

42. Kennedy, *Rise and Fall*, 171.

43. Kindleberger, *Financial History of Western Europe*, 63–66, 193, 216.

44. Kennedy, *Rise and Fall*, 152–53.

45. Maddison, *World Economy*, 128.

46. J. M. Roberts, *Europe 1880–1945*, 3rd ed. (Harlow, UK: Longman, 2001), 102; Kevin H. O'Rourke and Jeffrey G. Williamson, *Globalization and History: The Evolution of a Nineteenth-Century Atlantic Economy* (Cambridge, MA: Harvard University Press, 1999), 81–87.

47. David Brown, *Palmerston and the Politics of Foreign Policy* (Manchester, UK: Manchester University Press, 2002), 82–83.

48. D. K. Fieldhouse, "The Metropolitan Economics of Empire," in *The Oxford History of the British Empire: The Twentieth Century*, ed. Judith Brown and Wm. Roger Louis (New York: Oxford University Press, 1999), 100–102.

49. S. Herbert Frankel, *Capital Investment in Africa: Its Course and Effects* (London, 1938), quoted in J. H. Gann and Peter Duignan, *Burden of Empire: An Appraisal of Western Colonialism in Africa South of the Sahara* (Stanford, CA: Hoover Institution, 1967), 229.

50. Christopher Saunders and Iain R. Smith, "Southern Africa" in *The Oxford History of the British Empire: The Nineteenth Century*, ed. Andrew Porter (New York: Oxford University Press, 1999), 617.

51. Norman Gash, *Aristocracy and People: Britain, 1815–1865* (Cambridge, MA: Harvard University Press, 1979), 177–78.

52. Eric J. Hobsbawm, *The Pelican Economic History of Britain*, vol. 3, *Industry and Empire* (New York: Penguin, 1968), 340.

53. Gash, *Aristocracy and People*, 227–28.

54. K. Theodore Hoppen, *The Mid-Victorian Generation, 1846–1886* (New York: Oxford University Press, 1998), 306–7.

55. Hoppen, *Mid-Victorian Generation*, 330.

56. Hoppen, *Mid-Victorian Generation*, 308.

57. Hoppen, *Mid-Victorian Generation*, 598.

58. Hoppen, *Mid-Victorian Generation*, 600.

59. G. R. Searle, *A New England? Peace and War 1886–1918* (New York: Oxford University Press, 2004), 204.

60. Hoppen, *Mid-Victorian Generation,* 601.
61. Searle, *New England?,* 50.
62. Roberts, *Europe 1880–1945,* 101.
63. Searle, *New England?,* 333.
64. Hobsbawm, *Pelican Economic History of Britain,* 3:182.
65. Roberts, *Europe 1880–1945,* 25.
66. Searle, *New England?,* 627–28.
67. Searle, *New England?,* 631; Hobsbawm, *The Pelican Economic History of Britain,* 3:182.
68. Searle, *New England?,* 630.
69. Aaron L. Friedberg, *The Weary Titan: Britain and the Experience of Relative Decline, 1895–1905* (Princeton, NJ: Princeton University Press, 1988), 37.
70. Roberts, *Europe 1880–1945,* 23–24.
71. Roberts, *Europe 1880–1945,* 19; Searle, *A New England?,* 239.
72. Friedberg, *Weary Titan,* 131, table 3.1.
73. Searle, *New England?,* 247.
74. Searle, *New England?,* 281.
75. Chalmers Johnson, *The Sorrows of Empire: Militarism, Secrecy, and the End of the Republic* (New York: Owl Books, 2004), 82.
76. Searle, *New England?,* 283.
77. Friedberg, *Weary Titan,* 133, table 3.3.
78. Mitchell, *European Historical Statistics,* tables G3 and J1.

3

The Rise and Fall of American Hegemony, 1820–1973

As table 2.3 showed, the United States had only a 1.81 percent share of the world economy in 1820. Low population density, high life expectancy, and high per capita GDP suggested tremendous potential. In the nineteenth century, the United States gradually realized that potential, despite hindrances from obstructionists who tried to block its development. In 1888, the United States passed China and became the largest economy in the world. This was the result of both Chinese decline, as detailed in the last chapter, and American growth. Unlike China, the United States had the wealth and industrial base to translate military potential into military power. The turmoil in Europe from World War I enabled the United States to gain a hegemonic position by 1923. This position was lost when the Great Depression hit and the Soviet Union began its Stalin-era industrialization. Had the United States followed wiser policies in the 1920s, it might have been able to keep that hegemony.

Of the major economic players, only the United States and India were little damaged by World War II. The years after 1945 saw the high point of American hegemony. The United States possessed the wealthiest, most productive, and largest economy. It ranked fifth in life expectancy and ninth in infant mortality. It remade the international commercial system in its image. However, it frittered away these advantages by overemphasizing the military. Inevitably, this economic decline undermined the military itself. By 1973, the economic statistics indicate that the hegemony was lost. The Vietnam War came to symbolize the loss of this hegemony.

The United States in Relation to the World in 1820

1. England/Wales/Scotland	$2,121
2. Netherlands	1,821
2a. Britain and Ireland	1,707
3. Belgium (separate rating, but politically part of the Netherlands in 1820)	1,319
4. Switzerland	1,280
5. Denmark	1,274
6. United States	1,257
7. France	1,230
8. Sweden	1,198
9. "Italy"	1,117
10. Norway (separate rating, but politically joined with Sweden)	1,104
11. Spain	1,063
12. "Germany"	1,058

In 1820 the United States already had a higher GDP per capita than many areas.[1] Table 2.4 demonstrated that from 1700 to 1820, the United States doubled its wealth and productivity. Of the other great powers of Europe not listed, the Habsburg Empire had a per capita GDP of about $1,030, and Russia was around $689. In 1820, the United States had the advantages of the rich soils of the Mid-Atlantic and southeastern seaboards that had not suffered lengthy and intensive farming. The entire region had excellent water and mineral resources. The United States could feed itself and produce profitable cash crops such as cotton, whose production had exploded after the 1793 invention of the cotton gin. In 1820, around 72 percent of American population engaged in agriculture as opposed to 43 percent in the Netherlands and 37 percent in the United Kingdom.[2] Already in 1820, U.S. life expectancy was tied with that of Sweden, behind only the German lands and the United Kingdom and ahead of France, Japan, and the Netherlands.[3] This relative healthfulness promised upside potential in future productivity and wealth.

American Economic Growth, 1820–1870

Between 1820 and 1870, in its "proto-industrial" period, American GDP grew twice as fast as any European country. Only Australia, New Zealand, and Canada outstripped it and they were growing from virtually nothing.[4] Between 1820 and 1870, the area of the United States had grown by 70 percent, the population had quadrupled, life expectancy at birth for native-born

Americans had increased from thirty-nine to forty-four, the percentage of Americans working in agriculture had fallen from 72 percent to 53.5 percent, and 85,170 kilometers of railroad had been built.[5] By 1870, the per capita GDP ranks stood as follows:

1. Australia	3,645
2. England/Wales/Scotland	3,487
2a. Britain and Ireland	3,191
3. Netherlands	2,753
4. New Zealand	2,704
5. Belgium	2,697
6. United States	2,445
7. Switzerland	2,202
8. Denmark	2,003
9. France	1,876
10. "Germany"	1,821
11. Canada	1,695
12. Sweden	1,664

The United States was 73.64 percent of the British figure in 1820 and 76.62 percent of the British figure in 1870.[6] In some respects it seemed that the United States was standing still. On the other hand, it kept pace with a country going through its most dynamic stage of development in the Industrial Revolution. The United States was 19 percent ahead of Germany in 1820 and 34 percent ahead in 1870. In 1890, 38 percent of the American workforce was still farming.[7] Other nonindustrial countries of 1870 had fallen back considerably such as Spain, which had 62.27 percent of the British figure in 1820, but only 43.12 percent in 1870. The figures are also affected by Britain sloughing off the poorest people in Ireland and sending some of them to the United States in the potato famine of the 1840s.

Even in the colonial days, the level of education in the northern colonies was greater than in the United Kingdom. Within the United States, a gap opened between the north and south. The northern colonies had eight universities, the south only one.[8] Between 1825 and 1850 public schools were established to be the main centers of education.[9] By the mid-nineteenth century, the American school enrollment rate was highest in the world.[10] It passed Prussia, which had hit a ceiling of 77 percent of children between the age of five and fourteen in school in the 1840s.[11] The free public school movement began in New England in the 1820s. Gradually, northern states abolished school fees.[12] Significantly, there was no American gender gap in schooling till age sixteen.[13] In the 1850s, the overall literacy rate was 94 percent, while the white literacy rate in the South was only 80 percent and the slave literacy rate was but 10 percent.[14] Eighty percent of the South's labor force was agricultural which was enough of an imbalance to make the majority of the entire nation's workforce agricultural on the eve of the Civil War.[15] Massachusetts was the first state to enact compulsory elementary education in 1852. By 1900, only Iowa and the former slave states (save Kentucky) did not require eight- to fourteen-year-olds to attend school.[16] We do not have national education statistics for the United States before 1871. The first statistics of 1871 show 19 percent of the population enrolled in elementary schools.

There was a rapid expansion onto the rich and well-watered land of the Mississippi basin. By 1858, this entire area had achieved statehood. Between 1810 and 1830 slave plantations claimed the Mississippi Delta region. By 1850, there was population density of over eighteen persons per square mile all the way up the valley into southwestern Wisconsin. This in turn allowed for the harnessing of the Mississippi as a transportation hub. In 1816 80,000 tons of freight had reached New Orleans from the interior; this grew to over 542,000 tons in 1840.[17] Cotton production quadrupled from 1820 to 1840 and tripled from 1840 to 1860.[18] New York State built good roads and opened the Erie Canal in 1825. Pennsylvania, Ohio, and Indiana were also engaged in extensive canal building in the 1820s and 1830s.[19]

Why Did the United States Not Industrialize Earlier?

This explosion of land under cultivation, education, and transportation is sometimes called a "market revolution" and begs the question why the United States did not begin to industrialize in the 1830s and 1840s. The main answer was that even as it developed, a part of the country began to obstruct and hinder progress. This can be seen in the vital business of railroad construction. In 1820, U.S. per capita GDP was just above that of France and substantially above that of preunification Germany. In the years before the Civil War, the United States built more tracks but in terms of covering the country and creating a transportation hub, the United States lagged behind. Table 3.1 shows the total tracks laid and expresses it as a percentage of the total track ever used by that country. Between 1840 and 1845, France and Germany both surpassed the United States. There were similar issues with road construction. The government built a "National Road" from Cumberland, Maryland, to Wheeling, (West) Virginia, by 1818. In 1833, it reached Ohio even as its older parts decayed. In 1822, President James Monroe vetoed an appropriation to repair the road and demanded a constitutional amendment.[20] Later it was extended to Vandalia, Illinois, and to St. Louis, but the states were made responsible for its upkeep. States and foreign investors paid for most of the canals and railroads.[21] Obstructionists such as Nathaniel Macon of North Carolina and John Randolph of Virginia claimed that the precedent for the expansion of federal power could lead to the end of slavery.[22]

Education was also hindered by the refusal of the South to establish and fund common schools and teachers colleges.[23] While some southern cities such as Mobile, New Orleans, and Charleston created public schools, the only southern state to create free public schools was Louisiana. The Union had to impose free schools on the defeated Confederacy in the 1870s.[24] The one area where the obstructionists did not entirely prevail was the tariff, which was hiked in 1816 and 1828 ("the Tariff of Abominations") and again in 1832, but it is questionable to what degree the tariff protected American infant industries. John Quincy Adams's proposals for national projects of improvement came to nothing. Although the states south of the Mason-Dixon Line were increasingly outnumbered in wealth and population, the notorious three-fifths clause of the Constitution counting slaves for the purpose of apportionment of the House of Representatives and the Electoral College enabled the South to choose presidents and dominate the House. While it is true that cotton production was a major part of the American economy and "market," this only pointed the way to a banana republic, as was the fate of so many American nations. This obstructionism retarded American industrialization by about ten years; the Civil War that swept away the obstruction cost another five years. Most accounts of American history stress the growth in American numbers; the true measurement comes in comparison to other nations. If other nations progress more rapidly than the United States, then American progress is slower and in danger of stalling.

TABLE 3.1.
Length of Railroad Track as Percentage of All-Time Maximum (in thousands of kilometers)

Year	*USA*	*% Max*	*France*	*% Max*	*Germany*	*% Max*
1830	37	0.01%	31	0.07%	0	0.00%
1835	1,767	0.43%	141	0.33%	6	0.01%
1840	4,535	1.11%	410	0.96%	469	0.76%
1845	7,456	1.82%	875	2.05%	2,143	3.46%
1850	14,518	3.55%	2,915	6.84%	5,856	9.45%
1855	29,570	7.23%	5,037	11.82%	7,826	12.63%
1860	49,288	12.05%	9,167	21.52%	11,089	17.90%

Source: Mitchell, *European*, 315; *International: Americas*, 528.

The Civil War represented a stark choice: would the United States be a weak, hollowed-out, underdeveloped, and ignorant banana republic or a centralized industrial nation? The South lost its majority in the Senate with the admission of California in 1850 and would have lost its majority in the House of Representatives and the Electoral College with the reapportionment of the 1860s. While the North won the Civil War and swept away the obstruction, it did not take the next step and force the South to modernize. Most notoriously, "Jim Crow" discrimination reigned with no federal interference. Even as the United States democratized, many states of the former Confederacy went in the opposite direction.

As can be seen in table 3.2, a few states tried to hold out: North Carolina, Tennessee, Texas, and Virginia. The state with the lowest percentage of blacks, Texas, was the only state to show an increase in voting. For North Carolina, the turning point came with the November 10, 1898, massacre of the black population of Wilmington. In Virginia, there was an increase in voting participation thanks to the "Readjusters," an alliance of blacks and radical whites in the early 1880s. On November 3, 1883, racists massacred blacks in Danville and overthrew its elected and integrated government. The Readjusters were ousted by "electoral fraud and violence" in 1885. Virginia's blacks were effectively disenfranchised in 1902.[25] Less dramatically but steadily, discrimination fell over the other states. U.S. history textbooks celebrate the small triumphs of southern industrialization: conforming to the northern rail standard in 1886, producing 18 percent of U.S. pig iron by 1890, producing 23 percent of the nation's textiles by 1900.[26] These "triumphs" were pathetic. Discrimination, inequality, and ignorance remained the hallmarks of the old Confederacy. The survival of this recalcitrant remnant of the nineteenth-century obstructionists would be significant.

1888—the United States Becomes Dominant

The last chapter suggested that China lost its hegemonic position around 1855 in the chaos of the Taiping Rebellion. Its rapid decline continued, and China lost its dominant position in 1888.

Even in 1870, it was not entirely clear that the United States would take over dominance. It was sixth in per capita GDP. In gross domestic product, the United States was slightly behind that of Britain and well ahead of Russia. Part of the story from 1870 to 1888 is the relative decline of Britain and Russia. Paul Kennedy explains the Russian problem: low productivity from a population that was largely enserfed until 1861.[27] From 1861 to 1890, Russia was embroiled in a difficult transition to agricultural modernization and

TABLE 3.2.
Jim Crow Reflected in Election Statistics (presidential election turnout as percentage of total population)

	1876	*1880*	*1884*	*1888*	*1892*	*1896*	*1900*	*Change*	*Black% 1880*
Alabama	NA	12.04%	11.17%	11.50%	15.36%	11.64%	8.46%	-29.73%	47.53%
Arkansas	NA	14.12%	13.02%	14.03%	13.01%	12.17%	9.64%	-31.69%	26.25%
Florida	20.46%	19.15%	18.12%	17.05%	9.08%	10.10%	7.22%	-64.71%	47.01%
Georgia	13.24%	10.21%	8.50%	7.78%	12.06%	8.05%	5.33%	-59.75%	47.02%
Louisiana	19.12%	11.08%	10.58%	10.36%	10.33%	8.08%	4.91%	-74.29%	51.46%
Mississippi	16.82%	10.29%	9.91%	9.06%	4.09%	4.96%	3.70%	-77.98%	57.47%
N Carolina	18.93%	17.23%	17.77%	17.67%	17.37%	18.85%	15.41%	-18.58%	37.96%
S Carolina	21.49%	17.17%	8.54%	6.91%	6.12%	5.53%	3.79%	-82.34%	60.70%
Tennessee	15.91%	15.21%	15.68%	17.18%	14.99%	17.10%	13.50%	-15.11%	26.14%
Texas	12.41%	15.19%	16.83%	15.77%	11.64%	19.93%	19.83%	59.81%	24.71%
Virginia	17.18%	14.06%	17.99%	18.36%	17.65%	16.80%	14.25%	-17.07%	41.76%
Nation	18.9%	18.3%	17.8%	18.1%	19.1%	19.97%	18.2%	-3.70%	13.12%

Sources: World Almanac, 1928; Jack Salzman, David Lionel Smith, Cornel West, eds., *Encyclopedia of African-American Culture* (New York: Macmillan, 1996), 3029.

eventually industry. Investment capital, primarily from France, began to pour into Russia even as British investment capital poured into the United States. The Russian currency was not stabilized on the gold standard until 1897.

If this were simply a tale of Chinese, British, and Russian decline, then China would not have lost its dominance until about 1910 with potentially major consequences for East Asian history. The story is just as much about the United States building on the foundations laid in the 1820–1860 period, developing the more marginal regions of the Great Plains, linking the continent with a thick web of railroads, and building powerful international industries.

The first two columns in table 3.4 indicate that the rise of American hegemony had two distinct phases. The first phase, 1865 to 1890, was as much an increase in population as an increase in wealth. Most of these migrants came from Ireland, Britain, Scandinavia, and Germany. This meant most of them could already read and write and had some skills to contribute. They required land and raw materials to put this productivity to use. The nation's assets in turn became more valuable as this labor arrived. Transportation, primarily the railroad, allowed access to these assets and smooth move-

TABLE 3.3.
Share of World Economy, 1870–1910

	China	*Japan*	*USA*	*UK*	*Russia*	*Germany*
1870	17.23%	2.31%	8.93%	9.10%	7.59%	6.49%
1880	15.39%	2.47%	12.52%	8.93%	7.11%	6.99%
1890	13.53%	2.68%	14.17%	9.46%	6.61%	7.91%
1900	11.12%	2.63%	15.81%	8.92%	7.78%	8.52%
1910	9.42%	2.58%	18.39%	7.89%	8.63%	8.72%

Source: Derived from Maddison, *World Economy*.

TABLE 3.4.
U.S. Development Statistics, 1870–1910

Year	*Population (millions)*	*GDP Index (1870=100)*	*% engaged in industry*	*Steel production (thousand tons)*	*% of maximum railroad laid*
1870	38.558	100	22.68%	70	20.81%
1880	50.155	164	24.78%	1,267	36.68%
1890	62.948	219	28.10%	4,346	64.34%
1900	75.995	318	30.13%	10,352	76.05%
1910	91.972	469	31.70%	26,514	94.51%

Source: Mitchell, *International Statistics: The Americas*, 103, 315, 356.

ment of the fruits of this labor. The second part, 1890 to 1910, was mainly an increase in the per capita GDP. Electrification created a virtual "second industrial revolution." Agriculture mechanized. The new farmland that was added was mostly very marginal such as that of eastern Montana. The pace of population growth and migration slackened, and some spoke out against further immigration. The American system of education and training transformed lower-productivity immigrants into high-productivity workers. The final examination from Salina, Kansas, demonstrated the impressiveness of an 1895 education.[28] As Golden and Katz argue, the rise of the industrialized U.S. economy and parents' aspirations stimulated the high school movement from 1910 to 1940.[29] The rise of the modern corporation created a new managerial class working with new information technologies such as the typewriter.[30] From 1870 to 1910, the percentage of fourteen- to seventeen-year-olds attending high school rose from 2 percent to 10 percent. The number of female high school graduates rose from 9,000 in 1870 to 57,000 in 1900. The number of female college graduates rose from 1,378 in 1870 to 5,237 in 1900.[31] A somewhat different measure suggests that 6.5 percent of fifteen- to eighteen-year-olds were attending a public high school or a private academy in 1870.[32] In 1870, 0.13 percent of the U.S. population was attending university; by 1880, this had risen to 0.23 percent.[33] This jump in university attendance would not be matched until the 1960/1970 decade. For men born around 1900, 5 percent of their cohort graduated college, 10 percent of the 1920 cohort graduated college as the high school movement finished, and 20 percent of the 1940 cohort graduated.[34] The leading European countries, Britain and Germany, had a college attendance rate less than one-tenth that of the United States in 1900.[35]

Health showed a bifurcation. Native-born life expectancy fell from 1870 to 1880 then recovered from 1880 to 1890. Industrialization and urbanization clearly blighted the lives of many and increased infant mortality for which we are using the life-expectancy numbers as a proxy. From 1890 to 1910, however, the improved medical care and growth in personal wealth created a dramatic improvement from 45.2 to 53.1 in native-born life expectancy at birth.[36] Even as the per capita GDP and world share of the U.S. economy grew, it is clear that much was plowed back into education, transportation, and public health.

The First Era of Hegemony: 1923 to 1930

Table 3.5 shows the final part of the first rise of the United States to hegemony during the First World War and its aftermath. The numbers in the

TABLE 3.5.
Comparison of Shares of World Economy, 1910–1932

	USA	*China*	*Germany*	*India*	*UK*	*Russia*	*Dominance*	*Hegemony*
1910	18.39%	9.42%	9.60%	8.39%	7.89%	8.63%	1.916	66.51
1911	18.41%	9.19%	9.62%	8.10%	7.87%	8.65%	1.914	67.04
1912	18.70%	8.98%	9.74%	7.84%	7.75%	8.69%	1.920	68.22
1913	19.13%	8.92%	9.65%	7.55%	8.30%	8.59%	1.982	70.43
1914	18.72%	9.54%	7.92%	8.43%	8.48%	9.10%	1.962	70.48
1915	19.01%	9.51%	7.43%	8.13%	9.05%	8.54%	1.999	74.61
1916	20.56%	9.12%	7.13%	7.94%	8.79%	7.71%	2.254	85.81
1917	20.34%	9.35%	7.24%	7.92%	9.00%	7.43%	2.175	84.68
1918	22.23%	9.46%	7.28%	6.92%	9.08%	7.08%	2.350	93.32
1919	22.55%	9.60%	6.45%	7.92%	8.14%	6.76%	2.349	98.86
1920	22.54%	9.78%	7.08%	7.36%	7.71%	6.48%	2.305	96.57
1921	21.78%	9.76%	7.79%	7.83%	7.01%	6.66%	2.232	89.96
1922	21.86%	9.37%	8.06%	7.76%	7.01%	6.59%	2.333	91.01
1923	23.99%	9.18%	6.50%	7.28%	7.01%	6.65%	2.613	107.43
1924	23.68%	8.87%	6.91%	7.31%	6.99%	6.62%	2.670	105.71
1925	23.40%	8.65%	7.43%	7.15%	7.08%	6.65%	2.705	102.95
1926	24.32%	8.52%	6.95%	7.19%	6.65%	6.75%	2.854	109.45
1927	23.75%	8.32%	7.97%	6.95%	6.95%	6.78%	2.855	102.95
1928	23.43%	8.19%	7.96%	6.85%	6.86%	6.83%	2.861	101.96
1929	23.98%	7.97%	7.76%	6.89%	6.81%	6.77%	3.009	106.58
1930	22.60%	8.33%	7.54%	7.20%	7.00%	7.41%	2.713	97.08
1931	21.74%	8.76%	7.06%	7.51%	6.92%	7.88%	2.482	91.73
1932	19.65%	9.21%	6.67%	7.90%	7.26%	8.11%	2.134	81.91

Source: Derived from Maddison, *World Economy*.
Note: I have extrapolated the Chinese numbers from benchmarks using 0.7% per year growth from 1910 to 1913 and 0.95% per year growth from 1913 to 1932. Starting with the 1914 measurement, Alsace-Lorraine is not counted in the German number. Germany lost more territories with the 1919 peace settlement. Russia lost lands in 1918 and 1919. Starting with the 1921 measure, only Northern Ireland is included in the UK number.

table are approximate and the estimate for Alsace-Lorraine is removed from Germany's figure with the start of the war in 1914. China's figures are very approximate. The war removed western territories from Russia. The United Kingdom lost most of Ireland—about 5 percent of its GDP.[37] Nevertheless, these numbers are close enough to show the trend of the shifting balance of power. The American share of the world economy rose from 18 percent to 24 percent in the peak year of 1926. It extended its dominance to threefold by 1929 as the next largest economies were roughly even in size. In 1923, it achieved hegemony as it was larger than the next three economies combined.

There are three factors to consider. First was the impact of the war. As a neutral country for most of the conflict, the United States benefited considerably. Other neutrals such as Denmark, Sweden, and the Netherlands also gained simply by avoiding destruction, hardship, and large military budgets. Even when the United States entered the war, it only had a war economy for two years. The war led to the Bolshevik Revolution in Russia and the Communist repudiation of Russia's debt to France. The Treaty of Versailles confiscated Germany's international patents.

After the war came the inflation. The European powers had funded the war mainly by borrowing. Kennedy's estimates from Hardach are that \$82.4 billion in 1913 dollars were spent by the combatants.[38] Indirect costs boost this to \$260 billion.[39] The British and Americans provided the credits. This ended the persistent American deficit in trade, and surpluses regularly transferred capital from Europe to the United States. The United States had run a persistent trade surplus since 1876, but investments and invisible exports had maintained an overall deficit until the war.[40] After 1916, Germany had to print money to finance the war. Prices rose rapidly after 1920, especially in France, Italy, and Germany. The French invasion of the Ruhr triggered a hyperinflation in Germany in 1923, and the Germans had to establish a new currency. Several nations had to revalue their currencies.

Finally, the United States built on its lead in the 1920s. The percentage of the population enrolled in secondary schools jumped from 0.99 percent in 1910 to 2.07 percent in 1920 and 3.85 percent in 1930.[41] This was at a time when the population aged five to seventeen as a percentage of the total U.S. population was actually dropping.[42] This happened because of the rapid urbanization and the sharp decline of agriculture as a way of life that upset so many contemporary observers. By 1930, only 22 percent of the working population was still farming.[43] These shifts and educational enhancements allowed the United States to lead the next wave of industrial development. It was the center of the radio industry and the auto industry. Auto production in the United States tripled from 1916 to 1923.[44] This spun off countless subsidiary industries and stimulated road construction.[45]

In 1913, Britain, Germany, and the United States were roughly tied for the title of "most competitive nation in the world": each exported about the same value of goods. Between 1913 and 1929, the United States doubled its value of exports. As a percentage of the world's exports, the American share rose from 17.1 percent to 22.37 percent.[46] This occurred despite the Fordney-McCumber tariff of 1922. In per capita GDP in 1928 as expressed in 1990 dollars, the leading nations ranked as follows:

1.	United States	6,577
2.	Switzerland	6,095
3.	Netherlands	5,785
4.	Denmark	5,589
5.	Australia	5,220
6.	United Kingdom	5,115
7.	Canada	4,900
8.	Belgium	4,723
9.	Sweden	4,423
10.	France	4,390
11.	Germany	4,335
12.	Austria	3,682
13.	Italy	2,952

One should notice the sharp drop-off after Germany. Maddison estimated Japan to be at $1,992 in 1928. The U.S. per capita GDP had been 76.62 percent of the British figure in 1870; now it was at 128.58 percent.[47] The United States had gained dominance and hegemony; it was the wealthiest and most productive nation. It was highly industrialized with strong military potential, and it was setting the stage for the next economic surge.

The First Collapse of U.S. Hegemony: Causes and Consequences

By 1930 the first era of American hegemony had ended. The American fall came swiftly, and it came hard. While the Great Depression hit the entire world, the United States and Germany suffered the worst. This was not a coincidence. Some of the roots of the Depression lay in the very success of the United States. After the War, the government developed a series of related policies that could be termed "beggar thy neighbor." The end of the American trade deficit and its emergence as the world's largest creditor started with the war debts and continued through a series of loans extended abroad. In real terms the amount of international investment did not change appreciably from 1914 to 1938. But in 1914, American investment was only 8 percent of the total, while in 1938 it was 26 percent.[48] Without strong contrary actions, this led to a trend of gold flowing out of most other nations and lodging in the United States. Since the world was determined to get back to and remain on the gold standard, this created a critical shortage of capital for investment and other productive purposes. The United States in the 1920s should have pursued the following policies:

a. A greater presence abroad. After 1923, the United States withdrew all its troops from Europe. It refused to join the League of Nations. This had severe foreign policy repercussions that have often been discussed. However, it would have also moved American capital back into Europe as soldiers spent money and bases or other permanent structures rose. This would have been similar to the benefits of an American presence in Western Europe after 1945.
b. A move to open trade. The United States kept trade protection high until 1913, when the Underwood Tariff marked the first major move towards free trade. Imports needed to be stimulated if countries were to pay their debts. Instead in 1922, the United States enacted the Fordney-McCumber tariff. This not only depressed imports so that their value fell from 1925 to 1928, but it also likely inspired other countries to retaliate so that the spectacular growth of American exports stalled after 1925.[49]
c. Deficit spending. Another way to encourage spending and imports would have been for the government to borrow money and stimulate the economy. This money could have been used to imitate the early social-care policies of the advanced nations of Europe: old-age pensions, accident insurance, and health insurance. The government could have used this money to build a road system to accommodate the automobile or to expand the university system. Instead, the Harding administration and its successors cut taxes on the wealthy and ran a tight fiscal policy while keeping a fairly loose monetary policy.
d. Strike down Jim Crow. The black population was 9.7 percent of the American total in 1930.[50] In 1900, the death rate of the black population was 47 percent above the white rate. In 1925, it was 57 percent higher.[51] In 1922, the black infant mortality rate in registered states was 60 percent higher than the white rate. Only four states from the old Confederacy were included in the thirty registered states so the full numbers were certainly worse.[52] By the 1920s, African Americans were leaving the southern states in growing numbers. In 1910, 90 percent of them lived in the south; by 1930, this was down to 79 percent.[53]

I recognize that the above prescription was considered "politically impossible" in the 1920s. This decade saw the resurgence of the obstructionists who had lain stricken in the Confederate states. At a time when the United States had almost limitless wealth and needed to spend, the country fell into a torpor.

With foreign exchange fixed on a gold standard, and the government refusing to give more generous trade or fiscal policies, the only mechanism for international adjustments was interest rate policy. This was exacerbated when Britain and Germany, among others, came back on the gold standard at the prewar exchange rate.[54] They wished to pretend that the war had never happened. The result was that European exports were overpriced and unattractive unless industry forced down the price of labor in compensation. This led to deflation and brutal labor conflicts in Britain during the 1920s. The United States had to keep its interest rates very low relative to European rates to discourage gold flows.[55] This stimulated excessive domestic borrowing, most notoriously on the stock exchange.

The Great Depression came first to the farm. After the artificial war demand declined, farm prices fell steadily, even as productive farmers needed considerably more capital investment of machines and fertilizers. Agricultural productivity and urbanization led to much larger farms that required more investment. Easy interest rates encouraged borrowing, but when prices continued to fall worldwide, more and more farmers went bankrupt. Since farmers still made up 22 percent of the American workforce, this had a considerable impact and the government refused to bail them out. The only feasible response was to increase production, which forced prices lower. The plight of the farmers became much worse in the 1930s as drought stretched out over many years and dust bowls consumed the more marginal lands that had been farmed profitably since the 1870s.

The Hoover administration responded in the worst possible manner, as did Heinrich Brüning's government in Germany: they insisted on a balanced budget, raised taxes, cut spending, and let real interest rates rise to toxic levels. The United States, as the world leader in trade, also imposed the Smoot-Hawley tariff that led to worldwide retaliation. Even Britain finally abandoned free trade. One by one, nations relinquished the gold standard and devalued their currencies. In six years, from 1926 to 1932, the United States lost over one-fifth of its share of the world

TABLE 3.6.
Commodity Prices for Farm Goods Received by American Farmers, 1918–1933 (cents per pound or bushel)

Year	*Wheat*	*Corn*	*Oats*	*Beef*	*Hogs*	*Wool*	*Chickens*	*Cotton*
1918	201.6	137.0	76.3	8.33	15.26	58.1	18.4	29.3
1925	162.1	112.0	54.0	5.63	9.31	42.8	18.5	22.7
1926	158.1	69.6	40.0	6.31	10.99	38.9	20.9	17.4
1927	122.2	64.3	42.6	6.45	10.97	30.9	20.1	10.6
1928	115.2	75.2	49.3	8.48	7.81	33.2	19.6	18.6
1929	98.5	80.2	43.7	8.97	8.18	35.9	21.6	17.9
1930	107.5	77.3	43.1	8.69	8.80	27.4	19.8	15.8
1933	32.9	19.1	13.4	3.28	2.68	8.9	9.3	5.6

Sources: World Almanac 1928, 379; *World Almanac 1941*, 608.

economy. Often overlooked in the history of the Depression is the Soviet Union. Soviet economic figures for the Stalin era are hotly contested. Maddison derived his numbers (which table 3.5 is based upon) from official data. It is clear that the volume of Russian imports collapsed from 1931 to 1934. It imported 691 million new rubles' worth of goods in 1929, 830 in 1930, 867 in 1931, 552 in 1932, 273 in 1933, and 182 in 1934. Thus it fell 79 percent in three years. After that, its best year before the war was 245 million new rubles.[56] The ruinous policies of these three countries, which made up 38.5 percent of the world economy, go a long way to explain why the Great Depression was so bad.

Most upheavals hurt the country at the top that has benefited most from the system. The Depression also destabilized the fragile postwar security system. It undermined the governments of Germany and Japan and brought in more aggressive and expansionist regimes. The League of Nations never had much power behind it, but the budget austerity, the withdrawal of the United States from the world system, and general rise of unilateralism hollowed out the Geneva system. In 1931, Japan invaded Manchuria and began World War II in Asia.

The Impact of World War II

Ten years had changed the global balance. The U.S. per capita GDP had fallen about 6 percent. The Soviet Union had passed the other European nations

TABLE 3.7.
Comparison of the Major Combatants, 1938

	GDP (thousands 1990$)	*Per Capita GDP (1990$)*	*Steel Production (thousands tons)*
United States	800,300	6,134	28,805
Soviet Union	359,000	2,150	18,057
Germany	351,400	5,126	22,656
France	185,600	4,424	6,137
United Kingdom	284,200	5,983	10,565
Italy	140,800	3,244	2,323
Japan[a]	176,050	2,449	6,150
China[b]	320,500	778	NA

Sources: Maddison, *Chinese Economic Performance,* 158; Harrison, *Economics of World War II,* 3, 7, 10; Akira Hara, "Japan: Guns before Rice," in Harrison, *Economics of World War II,* 230, 277.
Notes:
[a]Hara estimates that Taiwan and Korea contributed another 15.7% to the above GDP value.
[b]Maddison, has $578 for 1933.

and had laid foundations for further growth: its railroad network was virtually complete and it had poured resources into health and education. It claimed that its literacy rate had grown from 30 percent in 1919 to 87 percent in 1939.[57] Kennedy is properly skeptical about the education numbers, but no one can deny that the Communist troops of 1941, with many defects, were healthier, better educated, and more organized than the tsar's troops of 1914.[58] Both the United Kingdom and Germany surged while France hardly moved. Some of this has to do with economic cycles: France's experience with the Depression began much later and reached the trough in 1935, when Germany had already left the Depression. Britain's stagnant 1920s left it room to catch up. Germany now had the ability to take on Britain and France at once. It could separately take on the USSR in a short war, but a long war that factored in the size and inaccessibility of the USSR would disfavor Germany. Japan and China were in a similar position. A short war would be no contest, but in a long conflict the Chinese (if given assistance) would make an invader pay dearly. And even in a weakened state with its hegemony gone, the United States could prevail in a one-on-one war. There were limits: the United States could not have overrun Russia or China. A German-Russian alliance would have been formidable, and a war between the United States and this alliance probably would have ended in a negotiated peace. With its low level of per capita GDP, China's offensive power was negligible. The Axis had only 83.5 percent of the American GDP. The three Axis countries were relatively small and accessible by water. Finally, Kennedy noted that the high rate of unemployment artificially lowered U.S. total GDP and per capita GDP. The American *per hour* productivity was a key number: if something happened to create full employment, both the total and per capita numbers would surge as the unemployed were absorbed into the economy.[59] This is precisely what happened when the war served as the catalyst. It accelerated because the forty-eight states suffered virtually no damage during the war.

The High Noon of U.S. Hegemony

At the end of the war, the United States had reached its peak. The war had devastated Germany, Russia, China, and Japan. It had damaged France and Britain. Meanwhile, the American economy virtually doubled. Military spending as a percentage of GDP peaked at 45 percent. Remarkably, this allowed "guns and ice cream." The civilian GDP remained steady at the 1938 level while the entire increase was plowed into military production. Civilian food consumption was mostly better in 1944 than in 1938. In the 1942–1945 period, the United States financed the budget with 47 percent taxes, 26 percent money creation, and 27 percent bond sales. Official military spending from 1942 to 1946 was $292 billion. The M3 supply rose by 96.65 percent ($78.0 billion) from 1942 to 1946 to pay for much of this, although federal taxes as a percentage of GDP reached its all-time peak of 21.15 percent.[60]

If we take 1950 as the first "normal" year where the worst of the war damage had been cleaned up, American hegemony had reached a high level. It was far higher than its 1923–1929 period. There were huge qualitative differences: in per capita GDP, the United States led by a wide margin.[61] It was an industrialized country with strong military power. The rankings in 1950 by the same measures as 1928 were as follows:

1.	United States	9,561
2.	Switzerland	9,064
3.	New Zealand	8,453
4.	Australia	7,493
5.	Canada	7,437
6.	Denmark	6,946
7.	United Kingdom	6,907
8.	Sweden	6,738
9.	Netherlands	5,996
10.	Norway	5,463
11.	Belgium	5,462
12.	France	5,270
13.	Fed. Rep. Germany	4,281
14.	Finland	4,253
15.	Austria	3,706

We would expect this margin to start shrinking as the other countries began to recover. By 1952 the American lead had *grown.* India's postcolonization problems were developing. Britain and France were in messy colonial entanglements. The Soviet Union was also sinking into late Stalin-era problems. While the post-1945 high was somewhat artificial, it was not entirely so. To American pundits, the "American century" would stretch on and

TABLE 3.8.
Shares of World Economy, 1950–1952

	USA	*USSR*	*China*	*India*	*UK*	*France*	*WGerm*	*Japan*	*Dom*	*Hege*
1950	27.28%	9.56%	4.50%	4.16%	6.52%	4.13%	4.01%	3.02%	2.85	133
1952	27.46%	9.22%	5.16%	3.96%	6.04%	4.06%	4.31%	3.41%	2.98	135

Source: Derived from Maddison, *World Economy.*

on, as confident as our hypothetical Chinese pundit had been in 1820. Yet within twenty years, the United States had lost its hegemony and suffered a humiliating military defeat.

To What Degree Was the End of Hegemony Ordained? To What Degree Could It Have Been Avoided?

It is for the 1950s and 1960s, not the 1990s, that one should talk of "hyper-power." The United States built a financial and trade system to its liking. It ordered the reconstruction of Western Europe to its specifications and threatened countries that defied this, such as Britain. It swept across the globe taking market after market and emerging for the first time as a trade superpower with a large percentage of its GDP dependent on selling exports. New York was the undisputed financial capital, the dollar the undisputed reserve currency. Even the USSR had to follow the rules of the dollar and gold. No conceivable alliance could challenge its power. And yet, some politicians and journalists wrote as if America's survival was at stake. Hegemony was not sufficient. They wished to break Russia and China, though wiser heads knew this was impossible. Robert Kagan sees this as a proof that the United States was never that powerful, but oddly includes the Suez Crisis of 1956 as an American defeat.[62] The United States did not demilitarize after World War II. In 1938, it had spent 1.3 percent of its GDP on the military; in 1947 that figure hit a low and began to rise again.[63] The economic figures also tell us that the fear in Europe was overblown. The USSR had dominance over the next greater power (Britain in 1950), *but it never had hegemony.* The patterns we have seen of GDP, per capita GDP, and industrial production tell us that an alliance of the Federal Republic of Germany, France, and the UK by itself could have fended off a Soviet attack as early as the 1950s. What about Soviet allies? What if one assumes the Warsaw Pact (formed in 1955) was a smoothly functioning alliance utterly obedient to Moscow with all of its soldiers willing to do their duty? This helps raise the CINC as measured by Penn State's Correlates of War project from 0.181 to 0.230. One must consider that if the United States was out of the picture, the three Western European countries would have had larger armies and military budgets that would have narrowed that CINC gap.

Any addition to this balance would come on the western side: Italy, Belgium, the Netherlands, Denmark, Norway. By the metrics that proved so prophetic for the two world wars, it seems clear that Western Europe could have defended itself. These figures, if one cares to run them, would be more lopsided for 1955, and even more so for 1960. And this is the *best-case scenario* for the Warsaw Pact, accepting all the Russian production numbers as

TABLE 3.9.
Comparison of British/French/West German Alliance vs. Warsaw Pact, 1950

	FRG/UK/France	*Warsaw Pact*
GDP (thousands 1990$)	781,696	720,761
Population (millions)	142,184	251,390
Per capita GDP (1990$)	5,498	2,867
Steel Production (thousands tons)	37,327	35,573
CINC	0.132	0.230

Sources: Maddison, *World Economy*; Mitchell, *European Statistics*; Correlates of War.

given and assuming perfect harmony in the Warsaw Pact alliance. For the same reasons as in the 1920s, a small American presence would have been helpful, but the overkill of the 1950s was unnecessary. These numbers are not secret. Those who tried to bring them up were denounced as Communists or sympathizers and ignored. The United States never had a real debate. It was simply pronounced that the USSR was militarily in the position that Germany was in at the beginning of 1938 (or 1939) and that it had the same ambition. The numbers above show this is false. Naturally, the Europeans did not mind putting the burden of defense across the Atlantic. As their economies grew, the percentage of their military spending fell steadily.

In order to maintain hegemony, the U.S. government would need to implement the following policies:

1. Keep pace or improve its health position in the world community. Health access for all, modern housing, and the completion of electrification would aid health and productivity.
2. Table 3.11 demonstrates that one of the major drags on infant mortality and life expectancy was the "Jim Crow" system of discrimination against

TABLE 3.10.
Comparative Military Spending as Percentage of GDP, 1950–1990

	1950	*1955*	*1960*	*1965*	*1970*	*1975*	*1980*	*1985*	*1990*
USA	4.7	9.1	8.3	7.4	7.6	5.7	4.9	6.1	5.0
France	5.5		6.5		4.2		4.0	4.0	3.5
FRG	4.4		4.0		3.3		3.3	3.4	2.8
Japan	0.0		1.1		0.8		1.0	1.0	0.9
UK	6.6		6.5		4.8	5.3	5.1		4.0

Sources: Roger Middleton, "Review Article: The Political Economy of Decline," *Journal of Contemporary History* 41, no. 3:580; *World Almanac*, various years.

nonwhites. Providing nonwhites health care equal to that for whites would have by itself greatly improved the U.S. position in health.
3. Modernize transportation on the short, medium, and long-distance modes. For long distance, air transport should become more rapid and available for people of modest means. The government needed to modernize the road system and make rail transport more rapid and available to those without airport facilities. It needed to improve and expand commuter and local mass transit.
4. Expand education access. It needed to eliminate the Jim Crow segregation and train people to the highest level in their chosen pursuit. Tuition costs should not be prohibitive. Culture and aesthetics should appeal to people's better natures and teach them to appreciate beauty.
5. Concentrated research would create "wonders" so that the United States would lead technologically.
6. An international trade and security system would protect American interests and safeguard economic expansion. Creation of an international market for American goods would rival the vast American domestic market.

Postwar American governments succeeded fully on the last three points, had some success on civil rights and transportation, and made some progress on health. In 1951, the leaders in female life expectancy at birth were:

Norway	72.70
U.S., White	72.03
Sweden	71.60
Netherlands	71.50
England/Wales	71.21
U.S., All	71.10
Switzerland	70.85
Canada	70.83
Australia	70.60
Denmark	70.10
France	69.30
Fed. Rep. Germany	68.48
Belgium	67.30
Austria	66.97
Soviet Union	65.00
Japan	61.50

The leaders in infant mortality in 1951 were:

Sweden	21.0
Australia	24.9
Netherlands	25.0
Iceland	26.0
Norway	28.0
U.S., White	29.6
England/Wales	30.0
Denmark	31.0
Switzerland	31.0
U.S., All	32.6
Canada	36.0
Luxemburg	41.7
Finland	44.0
France	52.0
Belgium	53.0
Fed. Rep. Germany	55.0
Japan	60.0
Austria	66.0
Soviet Union	81.0

These figures show that in both indicators of health, the United States was in the top ten.[64] Other countries surpassed the American health effort in the postwar years. In infant mortality, the United States was passed by Finland in 1960, Japan in 1963, France in 1964, East Germany in 1966, Luxemburg in 1967, Canada in 1973, and Belgium in 1977. In female life expectancy, the United States was passed by Australia in 1953, Denmark in 1955, Canada in 1957, France in 1958, Switzerland in 1960, and Japan in 1968. Under pressure from the civil rights movements, 28 percent of the difference in infant mortality was erased. Forty percent of the difference in life expectancy at birth was eliminated. The postwar era saw a modern housing stock with running water and electrical connections built. But the persistent health deficit began to affect other areas. From 1950 to 1973, the American lead in hourly productivity slipped. In 1950, hourly productivity had been 42.6 percent ahead of its nearest European rival (Switzerland). By 1973, it was only 21.7 percent ahead of the Dutch.[65]

Transportation was a mixed bag. There were undoubted successes. The government built most of the interstate highway system in these years. Civil aviation blossomed from 264 million miles in 1940 to 1,045 million miles in 1953 to 1,769 million miles in 1960 and 3,318 million miles in 1972.[66] However, bus and especially rail transport collapsed in this time frame.[67] Railroad, motor bus, and trolley service declined rapidly even as the total population rose and become more dispersed in suburbs. The number of

TABLE 3.11.
Development of White and Nonwhite U.S. Statistics on Infant Mortality and Life Expectancy at Birth

	Infant Mortality		*Proportion*	*Life Expectancy*		*Proportion*
	White	*Nonwhite*		*White*	*Nonwhite*	
1949				72.03	62.7	115
1950	27.85	53.7	193			
1951	29.6	52.3	177			
1952	29.1	56.8	195	72.7	63.7	114
1953				72.9	64.4	113
1954				73.6	65.8	112
1955						
1956				73.7	65.9	112
1957	26.05	50.4	193	73.5	65.2	113
1958				73.7	65.5	113
1959				73.9	66.2	112
1960	22.9	43.2	189			
1961				74.5	67	111
1962				74.4	66.8	111
1963				74.4	66.5	112
1964				74.6	67.2	111
1965	21.5	40.3	187	74.7	67.4	111
1966				74.7	67.4	111
1967	19.7	35.9	182	75.1	68.2	110
1968	19.2	34.5	180			
1969	18.4	32.9	179			
1970	17.8	30.9	174	75.6	69.4	109
1971	17.1	28.5	167	75.7	69.4	109
Improvement 1950–1971			13.56%			5.05%

Source: *Statistical Abstract of the United States, 1955, 1975.*

passengers carried by mass transit declined by 62 percent even as the population grew 34.3 percent.[68] Mass transit coverage on a per capita basis therefore fell 72 percent. The private automobile had to fill the gap. Americans drove 302 billion miles in 1940 and 1,121 billion miles in 1970. On a per capita basis, that is a rise of 141 percent.[69]

Educational access was made universal. Some progress was made after 1964 in reducing the Jim Crow gap as many school systems across the country were put under the supervision of federal judges. Educational authorities accommodated the huge baby boom from the early 1950s into the late 1970s. The percentage enrolled in high school peaked in 1979/1980 at 28.3 percent of the population aged five to seventeen.[70] Concentrated research led to "wonders" such as the moon landing and polio vaccine and a clear lead in technology, but the faltering of the supersonic passenger airplane was an ominous sign.

Building an international trade and security system was almost an unalloyed success, despite the overkill and acquisition of hundreds of bases.[71] Bretton Woods, the World Bank, the International Monetary Fund, and NATO are all instruments of American power. The Marshall Plan helped rebuild Western Europe and dampen the destructive rivalries. The General Agreement on Tariffs and Trade (GATT) and the later World Trade Organization regulated trade. U.S. foreign trade only accounted for 3.6 percent of its GDP in 1929, and even in 1973, it only accounted for 4.9 percent; but by 1998, it had ballooned to 10.1 percent of its GDP.[72]

It did a lot, but not enough, at a time when it had limitless resources. Inevitably, this took a toll on its standing in the world.

Imperial Overstretch, Faulty Policies, and the Energy Shocks

There are three aspects to consider here: share of the world economy, the dominance number, and the hegemony number. The dominance number changed somewhat as the Soviet Union rebuilt from the damage of World War II, but it did not shift significantly. Given the size of the nations and distance of areas from water, it seems clear that neither side had enough strength to conquer the other. The decline in the share of the world economy was more serious. In this twenty-year stretch, the American share returned to its 1922/1930 level. Some of this is due to the construction of the General Agreement on Tariffs and Trade, which was generally on an equitable basis, rather than an imposition of American hegemony. Thus American exports only grew at the pace of the United States and world economies and did not exceed them. This allowed West Germany and Japan to rebuild their export industries. It also reflects the failure to complete all the goals listed above. The failure to build a comprehensive health and transport system was serious.

Maddison shows that from 1950 to 1973, U.S. per capita GDP grew quite slowly, 2.45 percent/year.[73] Even countries untouched by the war such as Spain (which grew 5.79 percent) grew more quickly. It is not unreasonable to expect that the United States could have had a 3 percent annual growth in real per capita GDP as Norway and Switzerland did. Had the United States not had an extraordinarily high birth rate from 1946 to 1964, it would have lost its hegemony a number of years earlier. As it was, when the birth rate began

TABLE 3.12.
Comparative Shares of the World Economy, 1952–1973

	USA	*USSR*	*China*	*India*	*UK*	*France*	*WGerm*	*Japan*	*Dom*	*Hege*
1952	27.46%	9.22%	5.16%	3.96%	6.04%	4.06%	4.31%	3.41%	2.98	134.5
1953	27.33%	9.15%	5.18%	4.00%	5.97%	3.97%	4.46%	3.49%	2.99	134.6
1954	26.26%	9.28%	5.17%	4.03%	6.01%	4.03%	4.65%	3.56%	2.83	128.3
1955	26.44%	9.47%	5.12%	3.88%	5.86%	4.01%	4.86%	3.64%	2.79	129.2
1956	25.74%	9.92%	5.37%	3.92%	5.67%	4.02%	4.99%	3.74%	2.6	122.8
1957	25.27%	9.75%	5.46%	3.74%	5.55%	4.11%	5.10%	3.86%	2.59	121.7
1958	24.24%	10.15%	5.90%	3.90%	5.36%	4.08%	5.18%	3.96%	2.39	113.2
1959	24.87%	9.59%	5.78%	3.80%	5.33%	4.01%	5.32%	4.13%	2.59	120.1
1960	24.22%	9.98%	5.31%	3.87%	5.36%	4.08%	5.49%	4.44%	2.43	116.3
1961	23.97%	10.20%	4.21%	3.85%	5.35%	4.16%	5.54%	4.81%	2.35	113.6
1962	24.28%	10.01%	4.02%	3.76%	5.17%	4.24%	5.53%	5.00%	2.42	117.2
1963	24.27%	9.38%	4.23%	3.79%	5.14%	4.28%	5.47%	5.20%	2.59	121.1
1964	23.95%	9.88%	4.42%	3.80%	5.05%	4.25%	5.43%	5.42%	2.42	115.6
1965	24.21%	9.92%	4.69%	3.47%	4.92%	4.24%	5.43%	5.45%	2.44	116.4
1966	24.44%	9.85%	4.87%	3.32%	4.75%	4.22%	5.32%	5.71%	2.48	117.0
1967	24.16%	9.92%	4.56%	3.46%	4.69%	4.26%	5.16%	6.12%	2.44	113.9
1968	23.98%	9.95%	4.22%	3.37%	4.62%	4.21%	5.16%	6.54%	2.41	110.7
1969	23.42%	9.56%	4.38%	3.40%	4.46%	4.27%	5.23%	6.97%	2.45	107.7
1970	22.33%	9.79%	4.64%	3.40%	4.34%	4.29%	5.84%	7.34%	2.28	97.2
1971	22.10%	9.65%	4.67%	3.30%	4.25%	4.32%	5.18%	7.38%	2.29	99.5
1972	22.21%	9.26%	4.59%	3.14%	4.20%	4.31%	5.16%	7.64%	2.4	100.7
1973	22.02%	9.42%	4.61%	3.08%	4.21%	4.26%	5.07%	7.74%	2.34	99.1

Source: Derived from Maddison, *World Economy*.

to fall, there was some compensation by opening up immigration starting in 1965. The failure to make all the necessary investments in health care and transportation cost the nation dearly.

Imperial overstretch became a critical problem as shown by the percentage of U.S. GDP devoted to the official military budget.[74]

1950	4.73%
1951	6.02%
1952	11.24%
1953	12.18%
1954	11.41%
1955	9.07%
1956	8.67%
1957	8.81%
1958	8.95%
1959	8.71%
1960	8.31%
1961	8.80%
1962	8.53%
1963	8.36%
1964	7.50%
1965	7.43%
1966	7.45%
1967	8.73%
1968	9.15%
1969	8.55%
1970	7.59%
1971	7.24%

From 1950 to 1970 productivity grew 104.18 percent, while real per capita GDP grew 57.2 percent. Part of this discrepancy stems from the baby boom in the United States which yielded a large group of people who were not yet in the workforce. This big increase in the population helped sustain the size of GDP. The trend reversed itself from 1970 to 1998 as productivity grew 48.69 percent, while real per capita GDP grew 81.84 percent. However, regression analysis suggests that for every 100 basis points of GDP the military budget rises, it costs the GDP fours years out and takes 23 basis points from GDP growth. The increase that started with the Korean War took a piece out of economic growth from 1955 to 1959. Table 3.10 shows that during the 1950s, only France increased its military budget as a percentage of GDP, while Japan stayed at a peacetime level and the British and Germans cut their budgets. In

1950, the British and French military budgets had exceeded that of the United States as a percentage of their economies.

Starting in 1964, the military budget began a slight fall and this helped sustain hegemony, but by 1967 the war in Vietnam had gotten out of hand. The increase of almost one quarter in the military budget dealt a serious blow to the American competitive position. The government's decision to pay for the war with printed money worsened the problem: the M3 money supply rose $60 billion (10.28 percent) in 1967 and $59 billion (8.75 percent) in 1968. Compared to these figures, revenues rose only $18 billion and $4 billion respectively, and the national debt rose $7 billion and $21 billion respectively.[75] This would fuel part of the inflation of the 1970s.

The Energy Crisis

Another "bolt from the blue" was the explosive growth in oil prices. Much of the general postwar prosperity had been built on cheap petroleum. Global proved reserves increased eightfold from 1950 to 1973 while demand only increased fivefold. The 1969 world oil price was 65 percent below the 1947 level in real terms.[76] Even in nominal terms, the price had dropped 6 percent from 1950 to 1970 as a barrel of crude oil cost $2.88 and a gallon of gasoline (including taxes) cost thirty-five cents.[77] The development of the Texas oil fields in the 1930s turned the United States into the world's leading oil producer and exporter. It remained a net exporter until 1948. The ability to draw upon limitless reserves had been decisive in World War II. In 1950, the United States had produced 52 percent of all the petroleum in the world. In 1970, this production peaked at 3.5 billion barrels, which represented 21 percent of global production.[78] Had not Interior Secretary Walter Hickel so badly bungled oil production in Alaska and offshore California, this peak could have been delayed and occurred at a higher level.[79] This opened a 1.5 million barrel a day gap that had to be filled by Middle Eastern oil. This danger had long been projected and remedies prescribed (including import quotas to force a rise in the domestic price) to avoid it, but the politicians would not endorse any solution.[80]

What may have been the first event that signaled the waning of U.S. hegemony came in September 1969 when Muammar al-Qaddafi and about a dozen officers seized power in Libya while King Idris was out of the country.[81] The Nixon administration declined to act and indeed informed on anti-Qaddafi plots as Qaddafi evicted the British and Americans from their bases. Henry Kissinger blamed this debacle on the Foreign Service and the Middle East experts of the State Department.[82] In early 1970, Qaddafi demanded a rise of forty-four cents in the price paid for oil even as world demand was slumping.[83] Indeed, most oil-producing nations were begging to increase their production quotas. Libya did hold leverage over Occidental Petroleum, which was heavily invested in the country. When Occidental sought support from Exxon, that company would not move without antitrust relaxation from Nixon's Justice Department.[84] The surrender to Tripoli was quickly followed by similar demands from Iran, Iraq, Algeria, and Kuwait.[85] The American situation worsened as oil consumption grew rapidly in the United States from 1969 to 1973. Jack Anderson and James Boyd suggest that the overall policies of the Nixon Administration cost supply of about 9 million barrels a day, more than enough to weather the 1973 crisis.[86] When Nixon was inaugurated, the United States imported 13 percent of its oil, two-thirds of which came from the Americas. In 1973, it imported 26 percent. Of that 42 percent came from the Americas, and 33 percent came from Muslim nations of the Mediterranean and Middle East.[87] Well before the Yom Kippur War, the price of oil per barrel had risen from $1.40 to $5.[88] By the time Nixon left office in August 1974, the price was $12 a barrel.[89]

The Decline That Need Not Have Been

By 1973 the rankings in per capita GDP had changed.[90] They were:

1. Switzerland	18,204
2. United States	16,689
3. Denmark	13,945
4. Canada	13,838
5. Sweden	13,493
6. Fed. Rep. Germany	13,147
7. France	13,123
8. Netherlands	13,082
9. Australia	12,759
10. New Zealand	12,513
11. Belgium	12,170
12. United Kingdom	12,022
13. Japan	11,439
14. Norway	11,246
15. Austria	11,235
16. Finland	11,085

In 1969 or 1970, the American hegemony number fell below 100 for the first time since World War II.[91] The move to empire had a cumulative effect. If we assume that the military budget had been capped at 4.74 percent of GDP, we find the resulting gains in GDP would have led to a U.S. economy that was 18.7 percent larger and would have a share of 25.11 percent of the world economy with a hegemony number of 103 in 1973. Let us go a step further and assume that the proper investments had been made in education, health care, and transportation, enough at least so that the annual U.S. per capita GDP growth did not lag at 2.45 percent but kept pace with Norway and Switzerland at 3 percent while keeping the military budget capped as above (thus NATO and no more). The U.S. economy in 1973 would have been 33.5 percent larger than it was and would have had a hegemony number of 106.36. Finally, let us keep the 3 percent real annual per capita growth in GDP but assume that after 1950, the United States had reverted to a peacetime defense budget of 1 percent of GDP. What then? The U.S. economy would have been 54.57 percent bigger with a 30.39 percent share of the world economy and a hegemony number of 110.96. With a larger economy, the actual military budget for 1973 of $75 billion would have only been 3.7 percent of GDP. These counterfactuals are only meant as think-pieces, but one can imagine the United States extending its hegemony. Since the hegemony number did not slip below 90 until 2003, one may suggest that this could have been open-ended. The failures of 1950 to 1973 were critical. The end of hegemony was not an inevitable consequence of postwar recovery. Despite its considerable advantages, by 1973, the United States had given up the top slot in per capita GDP to a nation that had suffered no damage in World War II. Switzerland had not been forced to rebuild its manufacturing to a state-of-the-art level nor had it received massive amounts of American aid.

Notes

1. Angus Maddison, *The World Economy: A Millennial Perspective* (Paris: OECD, 2001), 90. The figures are in constant 1990 GK price purchasing parities.
2. Maddison, *World Economy*, 95.
3. Maddison, *World Economy*, 30.
4. Maddison, *World Economy*, 187.
5. *World Almanac 2011* (New York, 2010), 608; Brian Mitchell, *International Historical Statistics, 1750–2005: The Americas* (New York: Palgrave Macmillan, 2008); U.S. Bureau of the Census, *Statistical Abstract of the United States: 1955* (Washington, DC: Government Printing Office, 1955), 7; Maddison, *World Economy*, 30. Richard H. Steckel, "A History of the Standard of Living in the United States," posted February 1, 2010, accessed June 4, 2012, http://eh.net/encyclopedia/article/steckel.standard.living.us.
6. Maddison, *World Economy*, 185.

7. Maddison, *World Economy*, 95.
8. Maddison, *World Economy*, 107.
9. John M. Murrin, Paul E. Johnson, James M. McPherson, Gary Gerstle, Emily Rosenberg, and Norman L. Rosenberg, *Liberty, Equality, Power: A History of the American People*, compact 4th ed. (Belmont, CA: Thomson Wadsworth, 2006), 424.
10. Claudia Golden and Lawrence F. Katz, *The Race between Education and Technology* (Cambridge, MA: Harvard University Press, 2008), 140.
11. Golden and Katz, *Race between Education and Technology*, 408n.
12. Golden and Katz, *Race between Education and Technology*, 141–43.
13. Golden and Katz, *Race between Education and Technology*, 152.
14. Murrin et al., *Liberty, Equality, Power*, 536.
15. Murrin et al., *Liberty, Equality, Power*, 537.
16. "State Compulsory School Attendance Laws," accessed June 2, 2012, www.infoplease.com/ipa/AO112617.html.
17. John A. Garraty, *The American Nation: A History of the United States*, 7th ed. (New York, 1991: HarperCollins), 245.
18. From 300,000 bales to 1.2 million to 3.5 million. Garraty, *American Nation*, 238.
19. Garraty, *American Nation*, 247–49; Murrin et al., *Liberty, Equality, Power*, 349.
20. Murrin et al., *Liberty, Equality, Power*, 349. Daniel Walker Howe, *What God Hath Wrought: The Transformation of America, 1815–1848* (New York: Oxford University Press, 2007), 212, explains Monroe's long and contradictory veto message.
21. Murrin et al., *Liberty, Equality, Power*, 349.
22. Howe, *What God Hath Wrought*, 221–22.
23. Garraty, *American Nation*, 324.
24. Golden and Katz, *Race between Education and Technology*, 143–44.
25. Earl Lewis, "Virginia," in *Encyclopedia of African-American Culture*, 2747.
26. Murrin et al., *Liberty, Equality, Power*, 674.
27. Paul Kennedy, *The Rise and Fall of the Great Powers: Economic Change and Military Conflict from 1500 to 2000* (New York: Random House, 1987), 178.
28. "Put to the Test," accessed June 4, 2012, www.salina.com/1895test. While there is dispute as to whether this is an eighth-grade, high school, or teachers' exam, the document's provenance is unchallenged.
29. Golden and Katz, *Race between Education and Technology*, 166.
30. Golden and Katz, *Race between Education and Technology*, 172.
31. Murrin et al., *Liberty, Equality, Power*, 694.
32. Golden and Katz, *Race between Education and Technology*, 188.
33. Mitchell, *International Historical Statistics, 1750–2005*, 738.
34. Golden and Katz, *Race between Education and Technology*, 249.
35. Golden and Katz, *Race between Education and Technology*, 256.
36. From Steckel: 1850 38.3, 1860 41.8, 1870 44.0, 1880 39.4, 1890 45.2, 1900 47.8, 1910 53.1.
37. Maddison, *World Economy*, 247.
38. Kennedy, *Rise and Fall*, 274.
39. Kennedy, *Rise and Fall*, 279. This would be well over $5 trillion in 2012 dollars.
40. Mitchell, *International Historical Statistics, 1750–2005*, 424.

41. Mitchell, *International Historical Statistics, 1750–2005*, 738.
42. *World Almanac 2006*, 640.
43. Mitchell, *International Historical Statistics, 1750–2005*, 103.
44. Garraty, *American Nation*, 730.
45. Garraty, *American Nation*, 724.
46. Maddison, *World Economy*, 359.
47. Derived from Maddison, *World Economy*, 264; Maddison, *Monitoring*, 194, 196.
48. Maddison, *Monitoring*, 99.
49. Mitchell, *International Historical Statistics, 1750–2005*, 427.
50. *1955 Abstract*, 36.
51. *1955 Abstract*, 67.
52. *Chicago Daily News Almanac and Year-Book 1926* (Chicago, 1925), 286.
53. Golden and Katz, *Race between Education and Technology*, 206.
54. John A. Garraty, *The Great Depression* (New York: Anchor Press, 1987), 22; John Kenneth Galbraith, *The Age of Uncertainty* (Boston: Houghton Mifflin, 1977), 203.
55. Galbraith, *Age of Uncertainty*, 207–8.
56. Brian Mitchell, *European Historical Statistics*, abridged ed. (New York: Columbia University Press, 1978), 306.
57. James C. Riley, *Rising Life Expectancy: A Global History* (New York: Cambridge University Press, 2001), 211.
58. Kennedy, *Rise and Fall*, 323.
59. Kennedy, *Rise and Fall*, 331.
60. Hugh Rockoff, "The United States: From Ploughshares to Swords," in *The Economics of World War II: Six Great Powers in International Comparison*, ed. Mark Harrison (New York: Cambridge University Press, 1998), 83–110.
61. Maddison, *World Economy*, 178, 264, 279.
62. Robert Kagan, *The World America Made* (New York: Knopf, 2012), 110. The United States and the Soviet Union successfully demanded that Israel, France, and Britain pull their forces out of the Sinai Peninsula.
63. Rockoff, "United States: From Ploughshares to Swords," 83.
64. Mitchell, *European Historical Statistics*; Statistics Office of the United Nations in *Statistical Abstract of the United States, 1955*, 950.
65. Maddison, *World Economy*, 351.
66. *Statistical Abstract 1955*, 580; *1975*, 590.
67. *Statistical Abstract 1975*, 562.
68. *Statistical Abstract 1975*, 579.
69. *Statistical Abstract 1975*, 571.
70. *World Almanac 2007*, 402.
71. Chalmers Johnson, *The Sorrows of Empire: Militarism, Secrecy, and the End of the Republic* (New York: Owl Books, 2004), 32.
72. Maddison, *World Economy*, 363.
73. Maddison, *World Economy*, 265.
74. *World Almanac*, various years.
75. Federal Reserve historical data, FRB_H6, accessed June 13, 2012, www.federalreserve.gov/datadownload.

76. Jack Anderson with James Boyd, *Fiasco* (New York: Times Books, 1983), 52.
77. Anderson, *Fiasco*, 53n.
78. *Statistical Abstract 1975*, 686.
79. *Statistical Abstract 1975*, 58–74.
80. *Statistical Abstract 1975*, 85.
81. *Statistical Abstract 1975*, 195.
82. *Statistical Abstract 1975*, 207–14.
83. *Statistical Abstract 1975*, 221–24.
84. *Statistical Abstract 1975*, 242.
85. *Statistical Abstract 1975*, 256.
86. *Statistical Abstract 1975*, 289–290.
87. *Statistical Abstract 1975*, 533, 686.
88. Anderson, *Fiasco*, 308.
89. Anderson, *Fiasco*, 318.
90. Maddison, *World Economy*.
91. There is a slight divergence between the Maddison numbers and the Total Economy Database.

4

After U.S. Hegemony

Détente and the Five-Power Order

For a time after its hegemony had collapsed in the Vietnam debacle, it seemed that the United States could repair the problems that had caused its decline. The rising influence of Henry Kissinger brought a more realistic foreign policy by 1973. Kissinger recognized that the world was no longer bipolar in nature: Western Europe and Japan could stand on an equal footing with the United States and USSR, and the People's Republic of China had ended its long slide.[1] To the displeasure of Nixon and Kissinger, the Federal Republic of Germany embarked on its own foreign policy of *Ostpolitik* that went much further than American détente.[2] Richard Nixon's government oversaw the enactment of environmental measures and tried to get comprehensive health care. Amtrak emerged from the wreckage of mismanaged rail companies. Successive governments reduced the military budget, used the money for more productive purposes, and tried to get allies to share more of the military burden.

The cut of 150 basis points in the official military budget made it possible for the Nixon administration to propose reforms and improvements in environmental and health care policies.[3] U.S. military spending as a percentage of GDP developed as follows:

1971	7.24 percent
1972	6.62 percent

1973	5.70 percent
1974	5.66 percent
1975	5.69 percent
1976	5.30 percent
1977	5.20 percent
1978	4.97 percent
1979	4.98 percent
1980	4.88 percent
1981	5.42 percent
1982	6.05 percent
1983	6.29 percent
1984	6.56 percent
1985	6.12 percent
1986	6.26 percent
1987	6.05 percent
1988	5.78 percent
1989	5.67 percent

In the 1970s, the United States was able to keep pace with most other nations in health policies. It stabilized its hegemony number at between 94 and 99. Its dominance over the Soviet Union, which had slipped steadily in the 1950s and 1960s, grew after 1976.

The USSR was suffering its own problems of corruption, imperial overstretch, and overmilitarization. Once a major grain exporter, Russia could no longer feed itself because of inefficient agriculture and had to import large amounts of grain. The surge of oil prices should have benefited the USSR, but its inefficient drilling equipment left it ill-prepared. It needed to borrow massive credits from Western Europe and made political concessions in return. Most seriously, in 1974 it reported a great upsurge in infant mortality from 22.2 to 27.7. Within two years, the reported number had fallen below the 1973 figure, but that outlier led the French researcher Emmanuel Todd to write *La Chute finale* in 1976, predicting the coming collapse of the Russian empire.[4] In 1979, the Soviets entangled themselves in Afghanistan. Their inability to win decisively should have revealed the true state of Soviet power to all. In the last chapter I argued that the leading countries of Western Europe could have protected themselves against the Warsaw Pact in 1950. Table 4.2 shows the 1980 military balance.

The Warsaw Pact allies would add a bit to the figures. The Soviets would have the advantage of manpower and, superficially, hardware. The gap in CINC is stunning. The three-way coalition had about two-thirds of the

TABLE 4.1.
Comparative Shares of the World Economy, 1973–1982

	USA	*USSR*	*China*	*India*	*UK*	*France*	*WGerm*	*Japan*	*Dom*	*Hege*
1973	22.02%	9.42%	3.56%	3.08%	4.21%	4.26%	5.08%	7.74%	2.34	99.1
1974	21.48%	9.48%	3.54%	3.05%	4.06%	4.29%	4.98%	7.48%	2.27	97.8
1975	21.11%	9.37%	3.71%	3.27%	4.00%	4.20%	4.84%	7.60%	2.25	94.0
1976	21.19%	9.36%	3.52%	3.16%	3.90%	4.18%	4.86%	7.53%	2.26	97.0
1977	21.29%	9.21%	3.59%	3.27%	3.83%	4.16%	4.80%	7.56%	2.31	98.7
1978	21.56%	9.04%	3.82%	3.30%	3.80%	4.10%	4.74%	7.63%	2.39	99.8
1979	21.53%	8.69%	3.97%	3.03%	3.77%	4.09%	4.77%	7.77%	2.48	99.7
1980	21.12%	8.53%	4.02%	3.18%	3.64%	4.06%	4.72%	7.83%	2.48	97.8
1981	21.24%	8.45%	4.18%	3.31%	3.52%	4.03%	4.64%	7.93%	2.51	97.7
1982	20.61%	8.56%	4.45%	3.38%	3.54%	4.08%	4.54%	8.08%	2.41	97.3

Source: Total Economy Database 2009.
Note: The latest revisions have brought China's per capita GDP sharply down so that for this period, China would have a lower per capita GDP than war-torn Cambodia. I do not have better numbers, but I suspect that the U.S. hegemony number did not exceed 100 in the 1970s. Certainly, international politics did not indicate the presence of a hegemon.

TABLE 4.2.
Comparison of British/French/West German Alliance vs. Soviet Union, 1980

	France/FRG/UK	*Soviet Union*
GDP (in millions 1990$)	2,525,539	1,709,174
Population (thousands)	171,760	265,542
Per capita GDP (1990$)	14,764	6,437
Steel Production (thousand metric tons)	69,400	149,000
CINC	0.810	0.170

Sources: Maddison, *World Economy*; *World Almanac 1982*; Correlates of War.

Soviet CINC in 1950. Now it had five times the CINC. If one includes the entire Warsaw Pact, the CINC was only 0.219, one-quarter that of the leading European powers. The Soviets had much more to fear from a Western European invasion than the other way around. If Western Europe had to defend itself, it would have ramped up its heavy economy. The West had better trained soldiers and superior equipment. The Russians could have won neither a blitzkrieg-style war nor a long war of attrition in a straight-up conventional war. Virtually every alternative to this kind of war would benefit the West, not the USSR.

The Agenda of 1973

To maintain its position and to reestablish the hegemony that was not so far gone, the United States had to complete unfinished agenda items from the 1950s:

1. Improve its relative health position in the world community to return to the level of the 1950s. Health access for all.
2. Continue ending the Jim Crow legacy until health and education differences between the races were negligible.
3. Balance transportation development among long distance (air), medium distance (trains), and short distance (mass transit and automobiles).

New items of vital importance had appeared:

4. The entire infrastructure was aging: roads, railroads, electrical, gas, and water lines. The postwar housing boom had been built quickly and cheaply and out of inferior materials. By the 1990s, much of America's housing stock would start to deteriorate and have to be replaced.
5. A massive environmental cleanup.

6. Overhaul of education. There had to be a general across-the-board sustained improvement or at least replenishment of most of the pool of able teachers that was being drained as highly skilled women found new opportunities. Quick concentrated measures such as the post-Sputnik programs were failures. Even in math, science, and engineering, the United States produced neither the sufficient quality nor quantity as the "Apollo generation" that had been trained in the 1930s and 1940s retired.
7. Modernization of an aging industrial plant.
8. New "wonders" including cheap supersonic air transport, bullet trains for rapid transport, clean and safe technologies to replace fossil fuels. These wonders would serve economic and environmental purposes. Scientific advancement, research, and development should continue.
9. With the declining birthrate and an educational system unable to produce enough doctors and scientists, the United States would have to loosen immigration laws and provide incentives so that population growth could keep pace with the other major countries without sacrificing per capita GDP.

Productivity

As late as 1966, no major nation's average worker had been within 15 percent of the American worker's hourly productivity. In 1973, Dutch productivity passed that of the United States, and by 1982 Norway, France, and Belgium also had superior productivity. By 1994, Germany and Italy had surpassed the United States.[5] Much of this gain in productivity was plowed back into leisure time so that shorter work weeks, longer vacations, and a lower retirement age became the norm. This helped make workers more productive when they were on the job.

Health

The progress on health care policy was unsatisfactory, despite the United States leading the world in medical research. Nobel Prizes are an imperfect and lagging indicator: the United States did not have a scientist win a prize for physiology and medicine until 1930. They are still valid as some indicator for medical research and development.

1907–1945 42 scientists honored; 21 percent from United States.
1946–1975 68 scientists honored; 54 percent from United States.
1976–2005 68 scientists honored; 60 percent from United States.

TABLE 4.3.
American Comparison of White and Nonwhite
(ratio of nonwhite over white; higher number is lower quality)

Year	*Infant Mortality*	*Low Birth Weight*	*Female Life Expectancy*	*Reading Proficiency*	*Writing Proficiency*	*Math Proficiency*
1970	173.60	204.41	108.93			
1975		207.94	106.77			
1980	173.64	219.30	106.11	116.99		116.23
1985	169.89	221.43	105.21		111.59	
1986	176.40	223.21	105.21			110.82
1987	179.07	222.81	105.20			
1988	176.47	232.14	105.48	109.63	112.39	
1989	185.37	231.58	105.74			
1990	203.95	233.33	105.59			
1991	206.85	234.48	105.43			
1995	200.00	211.29	107.57		112.30	112.35
1997	196.67		106.96			
1998	198.33	200.00	106.95			
1999	205.17	198.48	106.96	113.81		
2000	200.00	200.00	106.52			
2007	235.71	188.89	105.21			

Sources: Birth Weight from *Statistical Abstract 1994*, 79; Life Expectancy, 87, uses "black and other" to keep consistency with older measures; *Statistical Abstract 2004–2005*, 67, 78; *Statistical Abstract 2011–2012*, 68, 76, 85. Education statistics from *Statistical Abstract 2004–2005*, 163, but eliminated in 2011–2012 Abstract.

A number who were trained in other countries did their Nobel work in American laboratories. In the era of hegemony, they developed valves, pacemakers, and open-heart surgery to fight heart disease. They developed vaccines against polio, whooping cough, and diphtheria and fought other childhood diseases such as measles and mumps.[6] The period after 1973 saw few such breakthroughs. There were bound to be diminishing returns, but one expected more with the growing amount of the economy that was devoted to health care. The percentage of American doctors trained outside of the United States and Canada rose from 17.5 percent in 1970 to 25 percent in 2002.[7] This was in keeping with agenda item number 9 listed above.

While most other nations provided universal health care and focused on preventive medicine, millions of Americans lived without coverage and the worldwide position of the United States in basic health continued to slip. By 1989, even the white U.S. rate had slipped out of the top ten.[8]

The female life expectancy at birth in 1989 in the modern world was ranked as follows:

1. Japan	81. 77
2. Switzerland	81.2
3. Netherlands	81
3. Iceland	81
3. Norway	81
3. Sweden	81
7. Italy	80
7. Australia	80
7. France	80
7. Canada	80
7. Greece	80
7. Spain	80
13. U.S., White	79.2
14. Denmark	79
14. Austria	79
14. Finland	79
17. U.S., All	78.5
18. Germany	78.1
19. England/Wales	78.03
20. Portugal	78
20. New Zealand	78
20. Jamaica	78
20. Luxemburg	78
20. Ireland	78
20. Malta	78
26. Singapore	77
27. Belgium	76.6
28. Taiwan	75.9
29. Soviet Union	74
30. China	70

The infant mortality per 1,000 births in 1989 was:

1. Japan	5
2. Finland	6
2. Netherlands	6
2. Iceland	6
2. Sweden	6
2. Ireland	6
7. Taiwan	6.3
8. Switzerland	6.9

9. Norway	7.1
10. Canada	7.3
11. Denmark	7.8
12. Italy	8
12. Austria	8
12. Luxemburg	8
15. Australia	8.1
15. U.S., White	8.1
17. France	8.2
18. Germany	8.3
19. Israel	9
19. Singapore	9
21. England/Wales	9.1
22. Belgium	9.4
23. U.S., All	9.8
24. New Zealand	10
25. Malta	10.1
26. Greece	11
26. Spain	11
28. Czechoslovakia	13
29. Portugal	15
30. Cuba	16
31. Soviet Union	25.2
32. China	33

Race Relations

While the Jim Crow laws were gone, the insidious impact of racism grew worse in some respects after 1970. The infant mortality proportion was 194.55 in 1980; it was 220.78 in 1990.[9] These were not anomalous statistics. The gap in infant mortality is worse than it was in 1950. The gap in lower birth weight rose steadily from 1970 to 1991 and then declined to about what it was in 1970. The gap in female life expectancy has not changed since 1975 although it is the least pronounced of the health differences. This made the health care problem worse. One should note that there was no marked difference among regions. Educational proficiency worsened from the late 1980s to the middle 1990s.

Environment

After some ineffective laws of the 1960s, the growing and obvious degradation of air and water led the government to act. The Clean Air Act of 1970 scored its biggest success by virtually eliminating lead pollution from the air. Sulfur dioxide and carbon monoxide emissions were cut in half, volatile organic compounds were cut by about one-third.[10] Spending on pollution control and abatement doubled in real terms from 1972 to 1991.[11] Progress on toxic waste, however, was glacial. The EPA reported 1,258 sites on its Superfund priority list in 1993. The list had grown to 1,284 ten years later.[12] While there has not been a proven cause for the rise in autism, allergies, and cancers in the United States, some suspect the growth of toxic wastes in the environment.

Education

While school graduation and retention rates rose steadily, complaints also grew that each high school graduating class on average knew less than the one before. Many college graduates would not have been able to pass the Salina, Kansas, final exam of 1895. In so far as standardized tests can measure abilities, the results were disastrous. From 1967 to 1991, the SAT verbal score fell from 543 to 498, the math score from 516 to 499. The ACT from 1967 to 1989 remained steady on English, declined in math from 20 to 17.1, declined in reading from 19.7 to 17.2, and rose a little on "science reasoning" from 20.8 to 21.2. The ACT was then reformulated to make later comparisons difficult. The SAT was similarly revamped. The National Assessment of Educational Progress Tests, on the other hand, mostly showed stability or slight improvements in most areas and age groups from 1980 to 1990.[13]

American education had long been able to take advantage of cheap female labor. Because of limited opportunities, many of the most talented women in the nation became teachers. As the century went on this situation began to change. Opportunities started to open up, and the proportion of female teachers dropped. The male to female ratio is one way to measure this. In 1920, 85.9 percent of classroom teachers were female. By 1950, this dropped to 78.7 percent. In 1960, it stood at 71 percent. In 1970, it was 67.6 percent.[14] The Soviet launching of *Sputnik* led to the National Defense Education Act (NDEA) of September 1958.[15] Despite its grand title, the act did little to enhance American abilities in science and foreign languages. In 1960, 18 percent of enrolled college students were taking a foreign language; in 1968 this was 15 percent. In 1974, it was 11 percent. Since 1983, it has hovered around 8 percent.[16] The NDEA's promotion of foreign language proficiency had the opposite effect. If one excludes college Spanish from the list, there are fewer total college students taking foreign languages than in 1968 despite the growth in general population and college population.

Higher education remained the one success story. Students came from across the world to American colleges and universities. From 1976 to 1993, foreign enrollment grew 149 percent. The largest volume growth was from Japan. Asian enrollment grew 200 percent, European enrollment by 314 percent, Latin American enrollment by 43 percent, and Canadian enrollment by 110 percent.[17] From 1993 to 2003, foreign student enrollment increased another 33 percent, with most of the increase coming from China, India, Korea, and Latin America.[18]

What Actually Happened in the 1980s

As shown in table 4.1, the United States remained just below the hegemony threshold in the 1970s, and its dominance number over the Soviet Union steadily increased. Amazingly, right-wing propaganda insisted in the late 1970s that NATO could lose either a conventional or nuclear war.[19] The Reagan Defense Department painted a grim picture:

> An army of 180 divisions compared to a total of 19 in the U.S. Army and Marines combined, 1,398 land-based intercontinental missiles compared to 1,040 in the United States. 50,000 tanks or almost ten times as many as are in the U.S. arsenal; 350 submarines of all types, compared to 121 in the U.S. Navy.[20]

A similar publication stated that the Warsaw Pact had 173 divisions, while NATO had but 84. It went on to state that NATO had lost its technological lead.[21] In retrospect, many recognize how nonsensical this was, but the facts were available at the time. Andrew Cockburn brilliantly demolished these arguments in his 1983 book *The Threat.* The Pentagon had earlier concluded that at least half of the Soviet divisions were empty and could never be filled because of the inefficiency of Soviet agriculture and the needs for a large farm workforce.[22] Of the alleged 5.8 million Soviet service members, a full two-thirds were construction workers, border guards manning air defense, or those stationed on the Chinese border.[23] The unopposed 1968 invasion of Czechoslovakia had been badly bungled with units becoming lost and hungry.[24] The 1979 invasion of Afghanistan had been a debacle that only stabilized when top-level European troops replaced the initial Asian forces. At the end of 1980, Leonid Brezhnev ordered the mobilization of troops on the Polish border. This was a shambles and Brezhnev had to purge the commanders.[25] He had to rely on the Polish army to take control of the country. Many of the Soviet tanks were broken; their crews received insufficient training, and the "modern" models performed worse than the older forms.[26] After Cockburn's book was published came the Mathias Rust incident where a German teenager flew a light plane into Red Square. Then came the defeat in Afghanistan. Kennedy's analysis of the grim problems of the USSR were precisely on target and the collapse four years later no great surprise for the enlightened.

TABLE 4.4.
Comparative Shares of the World Economy, 1981–1991

	USA	*USSR*	*China*	*India*	*UK*	*France*	*WGerm*	*Japan*	*Dom*	*Hege*
1981	21.24%	8.45%	4.18%	3.31%	3.52%	4.03%	4.64%	7.93%	2.51	97.7
1982	20.61%	8.56%	4.45%	3.38%	3.54%	4.08%	4.54%	8.08%	2.41	97.3
1983	20.87%	8.59%	4.69%	3.55%	3.56%	4.01%	4.50%	8.03%	2.43	97.9
1984	21.41%	8.32%	5.04%	3.53%	3.49%	3.90%	4.42%	7.98%	2.57	100.3
1985	21.50%	8.11%	5.38%	3.54%	3.49%	3.82%	4.36%	8.06%	2.65	99.8
1986	21.48%	8.16%	5.54%	3.57%	3.52%	3.77%	4.31%	8.01%	2.63	98.9
1987	21.45%	7.97%	5.91%	3.59%	3.56%	3.73%	4.22%	8.05%	2.66	97.8
1988	21.43%	7.80%	6.07%	3.81%	3.58%	3.74%	4.20%	8.19%	2.62	97.1
1989	21.49%	7.68%	5.98%	3.93%	3.54%	3.77%	4.21%	8.32%	2.58	97.8
1990	21.43%	7.34%	6.07%	4.06%	3.49%	3.79%	4.50%	8.57%	2.50	97.5
1991	21.11%	3.99%	6.39%	4.06%	3.40%	3.78%	4.86%	8.79%	2.40	105.4

Source: Derived from Total Economy Database, 2010.

The hike in the military budget from 1980 to 1984 coupled with anti-inflationary monetary policy sent the American economy into shock. When it sank to a 20.61 percent share of the world economy in 1982, that was the lowest level since the Depression or 1917. As the Soviet Union collapsed, the dominance number rose until 1987 when Japan passed the USSR and became the second-leading economy. In 1988, the hegemony number sank to 97.1, the same level as 1930. At the end of Reagan's term, the United States was weaker, not stronger than it had been when he took over. This was the context in which Kennedy wrote his conclusion to *The Rise and Fall of the Great Powers.* The USSR was on the brink, but the secondary American statistics were alarming, even if the research was not as complete in 1987 as it is today. Not only had the United States lost relative position in the world and to other leading economies in the 1980s, but the trade deficit, national debt, and budget deficits had all exploded. The health gap between white and nonwhite was back to Jim Crow levels. Productivity and per capita GDP by some measures had fallen out of the top ten.

Another ominous trend was the increase in the unproductive prisoner population in the United States. The Thirteenth Amendment to the Constitution allows prisoners to be treated as slaves. Some states of the former Confederacy used their prisoners precisely as slave substitutes. For many decades this population was negligible. But in the 1980s, the government imprisoned hundreds of thousands of Americans.[27]

1970	0.16 percent
1975	0.18 percent
1980	0.21 percent
1985	0.31 percent
1990	0.46 percent
1995	0.60 percent
2000	0.69 percent
2005	0.75 percent
2008	0.76 percent

In 1980, there were 474,000 prisoners in the United States. By 1988, this had doubled to 947,000. Black prisoners outnumbered white. The prison census indicates that of the prison population, about 95 percent were men, and 90 percent were between ages eighteen and forty-four, prime working age.[28]

From 1979 to 1990, wages lost about 18 percent of their real value. The Depression of 1982 saw millions out of work. The manufacturing sector collapsed; many were laid off in their fifties and would never get steady, well-paid work again. Unsurprisingly, the suicide rate among men jumped in the decade. The overall U.S. suicide rate rose 4.2 percent from 1980 to 1990; for white men it climbed 10.55 percent. The increase was mainly among white men aged thirty-five to forty-four and over fifty-five.[29]

Many criticized Paul Kennedy for turning his tools of analysis on the United States. Kennedy questioned if the United States could preserve (1) "a reasonable balance between the nation's perceived defense requirements and the means it possesses to maintain those commitments"; (2) "the technological and economic bases of its power from relative erosion in the face of the ever-shifting patterns of global production."[30]

What saved the United States to some degree was an open immigration policy. With the native birth rate falling after 1964, the gap was filled by foreign workers, many of them skilled. The immigrants also had a higher birth rate than those born in the United States. Had the door remained closed, the 1990 GDP would have been about 7.5 percent lower. The U.S. share would have been at about 20 percent of the world economy and the hegemony number would have been at around 90. Those would have been the lowest numbers since 1939.

The other major change was that the workforce encompassed more people who had been outside it before 1973: women in particular, but also senior citizens and teenagers. Before the end of hegemony, more women had been able to devote their time to raising children, keeping household affairs in order, and contributing to community affairs. As noted above, many women of the highest talents were only permitted to teach. Teenagers had more time for their studies, and senior citizens could enjoy retirement. This increase in the workforce and in working hours was needed to offset the relative decline in American hourly productivity. It was exacerbated when U.S. oil production declined, and the United States had to import more oil.

In 1960, 60 percent of the "noninstitutional population" was in the work force, including 1.6 percent in the military. By 1980, this rose to 64.1 percent, including 0.9 percent in the military. By 1990, this had grown to 66.6 percent. The 1960 to 1990 declines included: males 16–19 (58.6 percent to 55.7 percent); 20–24 (88.9 percent to 84.3 percent); 45–54 (94.3 percent to 90.7 percent); 55–64 (85.2 percent to 67.7 percent); 65+ (32.2 percent to 16.4 percent). Increases for women 16–19 (39.1 percent to 51.8 percent); 20–24 (46.1 percent to 71.6 percent); 25–34 (35.8 percent to 73.6 percent); 35–44 (43.1 percent to 76.5 percent); 45–54 (49.3 percent to 71.2 percent); 55–64 (36.7 percent to 45.3 percent). Only women 65+ saw a decline (10.5 percent to 8.7 percent). In absolute terms about 400,000 fewer 65+ men, and 500,000 more 65+ women were working. This was particularly notable for married women: in 1960, 31.7 percent of married women were in the labor force (a growth from 16.7 percent in 1940); it was 58.4 percent in 1990.[31] The fall in wages could only be balanced with a second household paycheck.

TABLE 4.5.
International Volume of Exports, 1973, a.k.a. "Most Competitive Nation in the World"

	Millions$	*Index (US=100)*
United States	71,404	100.00
Federal Republic of Germany	67,563	94.62
Japan	37,017	51.84
France	36,675	51.36
Britain	29,640	41.51
Netherlands	27,348	38.30
Canada	26,437	37.02
Italy	22,226	31.13
Soviet Union	21,458	30.05

Source: Maddison, *World Economy*, 359.

The Collapse of Manufacturing

As seen in table 4.1, the U.S. share of the world economy slipped in the 1970s, even as it maintained its dominance and hegemony numbers. This was reflected in per capita GDP and the productivity numbers. The United States slipped behind Switzerland in per capita GDP by 1973. Nixon's withdrawal from Bretton Woods and the move to floating currencies led to a steep fall of the dollar against most other major currencies. This angered the European Community and Japan which believed that Nixon was tolerating this so as to boost American exports and reverse the trade deficit that had opened on his watch. They need not have worried.

Table 4.6 shows the deteriorating competitive position in the 1960s. The one bright spot was the export of food, which greatly benefited from generous applications of hydrocarbon-based fertilizer. This allowed the yield per acre

TABLE 4.6.
Exports minus Imports by Broad End-Use Class, 1930–1973 (in millions of dollars)

	1960	*1965*	*1971*	*1973*
Food, feeds, beverages	-116	982	-319	7,983
Industrial supplies and materials	37	-2,107	-4,277	-23,123
Capital goods, except automotive	4,949	6,581	11,007	20,328
Automobile vehicles, parts, engines	633	990	-3,154	-3,526
Consumer goods (nonfood) except automotive	-505	-1,506	-5,716	-8,538
All other	531	1,060	-422	995

Source: *Statistical Abstract 1975*, 811.

to skyrocket. The capital goods row is somewhat misleading. In 1960 the ratio of exports to imports of capital goods was 10:1. In 1973 it was 3:1. In 1973, the United States enjoyed an export advantage in the following manufactured goods: synthetic rubber, coal, animal and vegetable oils and fats, chemicals in general, medicinal and pharmaceutical chemicals, agricultural machinery, tractors and parts, metalworking machinery, other nonelectrical machinery, electrical apparatus, rubber manufactures.[32] By 2006, the export surpluses it enjoyed were in airplanes, airplane parts, cosmetics, dye chemicals, plastics, miscellaneous chemicals, nonmonetary gold, printed materials, scientific instruments, ships and boats, spacecraft, specialized industrial machinery, coal, mineral fuels, cigarettes, crude fertilizers, scrap metal, and waste paper.[33] The only sectors that exceeded a $10 billion or greater surplus were airplanes, plastics, and garbage. Two of these three depend heavily on fossil fuels as do agricultural commodities, the largest nonmanufactured export.

The American manufacturing sector declined sharply. To take one typical industry, American steel production peaked in 1974 at 132.2 million tons produced. It lost 44 percent of that capacity by 1986. Its percentage of world steel production was cut in half from 1970 to 1986.[34] The big gainers were China and Brazil. Most of the loss came between 1980 to 1986 when the United States lost 27 percent of its steel manufacturing.[35] The Soviet Union and then Japan passed the United States as world's largest steel manufacturer in the late 1970s. Employment in the steel industry shrank 56 percent from 1979 to 1992.[36] This was not simply a matter of an aging infrastructure and it certainly was not because of overpaid union workers. Compared to other mature steel manufacturers of the western world, only the British suffered a collapse as severe as that of the Americans. Most peaked with the energy shock, but handled the subsequent decline better even if they were more dependent on imported energy and provided their workers with more pay and benefits than the United States. The trade deficit as a percentage of GDP reached historically high proportions. Demands grew for trade protection.

In 1980, U.S. manufacturing productivity was in the middle of the pack among the major nations: it trailed Canada, Denmark, Germany, Italy, Netherlands, and Sweden while leading Belgium, France, Japan, and the United Kingdom. By 1985, it trailed all except Denmark. In the same period, the United States was the stingiest in paying its manufacturing workers.[37] One might assume that the mass closings of the early 1980s would prune the least efficient factories and workers and be bound to raise manufacturing productivity, but it did not happen. A lot of workers lost their jobs forever, and those that remained had their remuneration slashed. One could suppose that they retaliated by giving a minimal effort, thus leading to a downward cycle. In 1995, when the dollar hit a trough,

TABLE 4.7.
American Steel Manufacturing Compared to Similar Economies (in thousands of tons)

Nation	*Peak Year*	*Peak Production*	*1986 Production*	*Percentage of Peak*	*Notes*
United States	1974	132,196	74,032	56.00%	
Canada	1979	16,078	14,081	87.58%	New peaks in 2000 and 2001
United Kingdom	1970	28,291	14,725	52.05%	
Belgium	1974	16,224	9,803	60.42%	
France	1974	27,023	17,865	66.11%	
West Germany	1974	53,232	37,134	69.76%	
Italy	1980	26,501	22,882	86.34%	New peak in 2000
Sweden	1974	5,973	4,719	79.01%	
Japan	1973	119,322	98,275	82.36%	
Non-U.S. average		36,580.5	27,435.5	75.00%	

Sources: Correlates of War; *World Almanac*, various.
Note: After 2003, the *World Almanac* no longer printed steel production data.

TABLE 4.8.
International Volume of Exports, 1990, a.k.a. "Most Competitive Nation in the World"

	Millions$	*Index (Germany=100)*
Germany	398,000	100.00
United States	394,030	99.00
Japan	287,000	72.11
France	216,000	54.27
Britain	185,326	46.56
Italy	170,383	42.81
Netherlands	131,787	33.11
Canada	127,634	32.07
Soviet Union	104,177	26.18

Source: *World Almanac 1992*.

manufacturing workers were being paid $17.19 in the United States, $23.82 in Japan, and $31.58 in Germany.[38]

This export problem stemmed in part from a strong dollar from 1981 to 1985, but the fall in productivity could be measured in other ways. Per capita GDP is one measurement of the broadest productivity of a population. Even though the average American was working more hours each year than most other citizens and a high proportion of Americans was employed, the United States still fell behind.[39] The 1981 rankings for per capita GDP were:

1.	Switzerland	18,946
2.	United States	18,856
3.	Canada	16,472
4.	FR Germany	15,859
5.	France	15,173
6.	Norway	15,221
7.	Denmark	15,095
8.	Sweden	14,917
9.	Australia	14,661
10.	Netherlands	14,524
11.	Belgium	14,276
12.	Japan	13,754
13.	Austria	13,710
14.	Finland	13,134
15.	New Zealand	13,000
16.	UK	12,754

By 1990, the per capita GDP picture had changed dramatically as shown in table 4.9. The Geary-Khanis Purchasing Power Parities were kinder to the United States. Indeed the numbers are so different that they cast doubt on this measurement.

The Hyperpower Illusion and the Revolutions of 1989

The revolutions of 1989 to 1991 brought unexpected change. They shook Western Europe from the course of development outlined in the 1987 Single European Act. The nations of East-Central Europe needed massive foreign assistance. The Federal Republic of Germany swallowed its eastern neighbor which hardly added any GDP. It had to scrap and remake the entire economy of the former German Democratic Republic (GDR). Many in the GDR lost their jobs and never regained anything comparable in pay. The environmental damage found in the east was awesome. On top of that came the collapse of the Soviet Union. Now came hundreds of millions of people who also required massive assistance. Germany for a time yielded its position as most competitive nation in the world. Currencies had to retrench with the British pound sterling losing one-quarter of its value against the dollar; this was an indication of the hollowing-out of the British economy that had occurred in

TABLE 4.9.
Two Measures of Wealth and Productivity, 1990

	GDP/capita	*PPP (Geary-Khanis)*
1. Switzerland	35,920	21,616
2. Sweden	27,490	17,680
3. Japan	26,440	18,789
4. Finland	25,970	16,868
5. FR Germany	24,260	18,691
6. Denmark	24,000	18,463
7. Norway	23,810	18,470
8. United States	23,020	23,214
9. Canada	21,450	18,933
10. France	20,840	18,093
11. Austria	20,480	16,881
12. Italy	19,440	16,320
13. Belgium	19,150	17,194
14. Netherlands	19,010	17,267
15. UK	17,850	16,411
16. Australia	16,690	17,043
17. New Zealand	13,687	13,825

Sources: Statistical Abstract 1994, 862; Maddison, *World Economy*, 276–304.

the 1980s and was reflected in table 4.7. This occurred despite the bounty of North Sea oil.

The immediate response of the American government was to declare that it had "won" something and could ignore all the mounting problems of the late 1980s. The United States led a war against Saddam Hussein in 1991 and not surprisingly defeated his undertrained and impoverished army. Wisely, there was no attempt to conquer Iraq itself.

The Clinton Stabilization

Bill Clinton's defeat of George H.W. Bush in 1992 ended the talk of a hyper-power imposing a "new world order." Clinton accelerated the long-overdue reduction of the military. He attempted to put more money into transportation, education, and health care, but Congress blocked or diverted much of this planning. In 1993, the military budget finally fell below its 1950 baseline of national defense plus NATO.

1990	4.99 percent
1991	4.38 percent
1992	4.76 percent
1993	4.38 percent
1994	4.08 percent
1995	3.70 percent
1996	3.33 percent
1997	3.18 percent
1998	3.01 percent
1999	2.81 percent
2000	2.86 percent
2001	2.87 percent

With the usual four-year lag time, the economy began to perk up in 1994, four years after the military budget was more than 100 basis points down from its Reagan high. By 1995, Clinton had reduced it a further hundred basis points from its Bush level and squeezed a second hundred basis points out by 1999, ensuring decent growth through 2003. Although he did not get the investment funds he requested, he was able to get the budget deficit under control. Real interest rates charged as an insurance premium on U.S. bonds had been growing and now reversed course. U.S. sovereign debt sold well at auction by 2000.

1. United States	27,331
2. Norway	23,660
3. Denmark	22,123
4. Switzerland	21,367
5. Canada	20,559
6. Japan	20,410
7. Australia	20,390
8. Netherlands	20,224
9. France	19,558
10. Belgium	19,442
11. Austria	18,905
12. Sweden	18,685
13. UK	18,714
14. Finland	18,324
15. Ireland	18,183
16. FR Germany	17,799
17. Italy	17,759
18. New Zealand	14,779

These numbers are from the GK PPP and the same caveats apply as earlier, but in 1990 the GK PPP had the U.S. 7 percent ahead of the second-richest country; here it is 15.5 percent.[40]

There was steady progress on infant mortality as it fell from 8.5 to 6.9 from 1992 to 2000. Life expectancy hardly budged, going from 78.9 to 79.5. Unemployment fell, and wages rose with a minimum wage increase in 1997 kicking off a consumer spending spree that powered the growth at the end of the decade. Meanwhile Europe was still digesting the revolutions of 1989 and Japan sank into a funk because of its restrictive immigration policy and the aging of its population. By 1998, the United States had made a remarkable comeback both in its share of the world economy and in its per capita GDP. Through a series of trade agreements, the United States had vastly increased its export market so that exports now equaled about 20 percent of GDP.

On the Jim Crow front, real gains were made in closing the gap in low birth weight but the achievements in infant mortality were not regained and the gap in life expectancy remained about what it was.

There was also a move towards greater equality. The census bureau releases figures on the richest five percent in American society and the rest broken down by quintiles. Table 4.11 shows that the ratio between richest and poorest 20 percent was 11.14 in 1967; 10.79 in 1980; 13.73 in 1994 and 15.37 in 2010. The ratio between the richest 5 percent and poorest 20 percent was 17.57 in 1967; 16.12 in 1980; 23.73 in 1994; and 26.07 in 2010. The stabilization was due to the robust economy which created jobs even for the poorest in society and gave wage increases. The increase in the minimum wage starting in 1997 had a ripple effect on the wage structure. The economy was robust because of steady reduction in military spending. The move toward greater equality encouraged consumer spending and investment. Trade pacts and productivity improvements also led to a boom in exports. By 2000, the suicide rate had plunged 16.1 percent. For men, it had fallen 19.5 percent.[41] The period from 1994 to 2000 saw wealth distributed across the board. From 2000 to 2010, there was a new burst of inequality moderated by the sharp decline of the stock market from 2007 to 2009.

Conclusion

After hegemony, the United States had a mixed record. In the 1970s and 1990s, there were notable successes by both Republican and Democratic administrations. Of the nine-part agenda of 1973, there was measurable progress only

TABLE 4.10.
Comparative Shares of the World Economy, 1991–2001

	USA	*Russia*	*China*	*India*	*UK*	*France*	*Germany*	*Japan*	*Dom*	*Hege*
1991	21.11%	3.99%	6.39%	4.06%	3.40%	3.78%	4.86%	8.79%	2.40	105.3
1992	21.40%	3.34%	6.87%	4.20%	3.34%	3.76%	4.87%	8.70%	2.46	104.7
1993	21.56%	2.99%	7.38%	4.34%	3.34%	3.65%	4.73%	8.55%	2.52	104.4
1994	21.71%	2.52%	7.86%	4.47%	3.37%	3.60%	4.70%	8.32%	2.61	104.0
1995	21.53%	2.34%	8.75%	4.64%	3.36%	3.54%	4.63%	8.17%	2.46	99.9
1996	21.50%	2.18%	8.59%	4.82%	3.32%	3.43%	4.49%	8.25%	2.50	99.3
1997	21.60%	2.12%	8.70%	4.83%	3.30%	3.41%	4.40%	7.92%	2.48	100.7
1998	22.05%	1.96%	8.53%	5.04%	3.34%	3.45%	4.39%	7.58%	2.58	104.3
1999	21.62%	1.95%	8.50%	5.02%	3.24%	3.33%	4.19%	7.09%	2.54	104.9
2000	21.43%	2.04%	8.83%	4.99%	3.20%	3.30%	4.12%	6.94%	2.43	103.2
2001	21.03%	2.08%	9.48%	5.12%	3.19%	3.26%	4.05%	6.75%	2.22	98.5

Source: Derived from the Conference Board's Total Economy Database, 2010.
Note: In table 5.1 the major adjustment of the TED in 2011 and 2012 that opened a 10 percent difference. Whether the United States lost hegemony for good in 2001 or 2003 is immaterial to my argument. Figure 5.1 matches table 5.1, not this table.

TABLE 4.11.
U.S. Equality and Inequality: Growth in Household Income between Selected Years

	1967–1980	*1980–1994*	*1994–2010*
Richest 5%	9.10%	52.12%	8.03%
Richest 20%	15.17%	31.58%	10.06%
2nd Fifth	16.24%	11.59%	7.81%
3rd Fifth	10.40%	5.65%	4.66%
4th Fifth	6.81%	3.49%	2.39%
Poorest 20%	18.90%	3.35%	-1.68%
Ratio Richest 20%/Poorest 20%	0.80	9.42	INF
Ratio Richest 5%/Poorest 20%	0.48	15.55	INF

Source: www.census.gov/www/income/data/historical/inequality/H03AR_2010.xls. Accessed June 3, 2012.

on items five (environmental cleanup) and nine (relaxed immigration standards). The lost decade of the 1980s devastated the American manufacturing base and created serious long-term problems. But going into 2000 the way seemed clear for continued development and American dominance.

Notes

1. "In economic terms there are at least five groupings." Kissinger quoted in Kennedy, 408. *Foreign Relations of the United States, 1969–1976*, vol. 1, *Foundations of Foreign Policy, 1969–1972* (Washington, DC: Government Printing Office, 2003) contains a number of documents which the State Department's historian has summarized in www.state.gov/historicaldocuments/frus1969-76v01/summary (accessed June 3, 2012).

2. Holger Klitzing, "To Grin and Bear It: The Nixon Administration and *Ostpolitik*," in Carole Fink and Bernd Schaefer, eds., *Ostpolitik, 1969–1974: European and Global Responses* (New York: Cambridge University Press, 2009), 90–110.

3. *World Almanac*, various.

4. Emmanuel Todd, *After the Empire: The Breakdown of the American Order* (New York: Columbia University Press, 2003), xv.

5. Derived from Angus Maddison, *The World Economy: A Millennial Perspective* (Paris: OECD, 2001).

6. James T. Patterson, *Grand Expectations: The United States, 1945–1974* (New York: Oxford University Press, 1996), 318–19.

7. U.S. Bureau of the Census, *Statistical Abstract of the United States, 1994* (Washington, DC: Government Printing Office, 1994), 121; *Statistical Abstract of the United States, 2004–2005* (Washington, DC: Government Printing Office, 2004), 107. It was still 25 percent in 2008.

8. *World Almanac 1992.*

9. *Statistical Abstract 1994*, 92.
10. *Statistical Abstract 1994*, 231; *Statistical Abstract 2004–2005*, 221; *World Almanac 2007*, 285.
11. *Statistical Abstract 1994*, 236.
12. *Statistical Abstract 1994*, 236; *Statistical Abstract 2004–2005*, 225; *World Almanac 2007*, 286.
13. *Statistical Abstract 1994*, 174–75; *Statistical Abstract 2004*, 162–63.
14. *Statistical Abstract 1975*, 124. After a numbers of years of absence, a comparable number in *2011–12 Abstract*, 164, seems to equal 76 percent.
15. Patterson, 421.
16. *Statistical Abstract 1975*, 114; *Statistical Abstract 1994*, 156, 186; *Statistical Abstract 2004–2005*, 169, 172.
17. *Statistical Abstract 1994*, 187.
18. *Statistical Abstract 2004*, 171.
19. For example, Norman Podhoretz, *The Present Danger: Do We Have the Will to Reverse the Decline of American Power?* (New York: Simon and Schuster, 1980).
20. Defense Department's *Soviet Military Power, 1981* quoted in Andrew Cockburn, *The Threat: Inside the Soviet Military Machine* (New York: Vintage Books, 1984), 7.
21. NATO, *Force Comparisons 1982*, from Cockburn, *Threat*, 163.
22. Cockburn, *Threat*, 161.
23. Cockburn, *Threat*, 164–65.
24. Cockburn, *Threat*, 175.
25. Cockburn, *Threat*, 112–13.
26. Cockburn, *Threat*, 254.
27. *Statistical Abstract 1994*, 215; *Statistical Abstract 2011–12*, 215.
28. *Statistical Abstract 1994*, 215.
29. *Statistical Abstract 1994*, 101.
30. Paul Kennedy, *The Rise and Fall of the Great Powers: Economic Change and Military Conflict from 1500 to 2000* (New York: Random House, 1987), 514–15.
31. *Statistical Abstract 1975*, 344, 346; *Statistical Abstract 1994*, 395, 401.
32. *World Almanac 1975*, 123.
33. *World Almanac 2008*, 68.
34. *Statistical Abstract 1994*, 770.
35. *Statistical Abstract 1994*, 874.
36. *Statistical Abstract 1994*, 413.
37. *Statistical Abstract 1994*, 873.
38. Robert Brenner, *The Boom and the Bubble: The US in the World Economy* (London: Verso, 2002), 61.
39. Maddison, *World Economy*, 304.
40. Maddison, *World Economy*, 276–304.
41. *World Almanac 2004*, 81.

5

The End of U.S. Dominance?

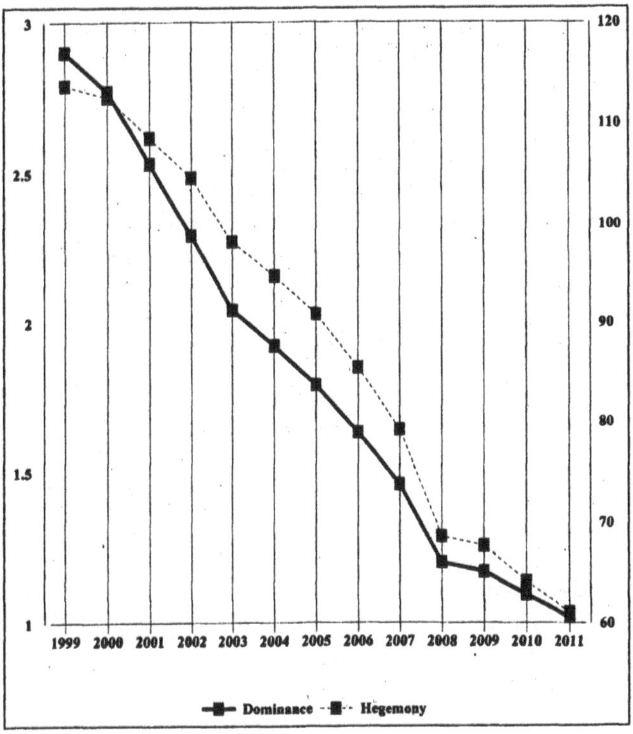

Figure 5.1 U.S. Dominance and Hegemony, 1999–2011

On October 25, 2000, the United States seemed to be on the upswing. The Revolutions of 1989 had sidelined European competition and forced Western Europe to pour billions in developing the east on top of the bad loans it had to swallow from the communist days. Crony capitalism, xenophobia, and an aging population had stopped Japan's march forward. The Nikkei index had lost two-thirds of its value and showed no sign of real recovery. The United States had aggressively increased its export sector and was again the most competitive nation in the world. It had regained the hegemony lost in the 1980s and had a steady dominance number as its economy was about two-and-a-half times the size of the next largest. There was at least some promise that attention had turned to the future and that health and education were at the top of the agenda. The American stock market had rushed forward and then peaked in March 2000. It was becoming clear that much of the Internet sector would never make money and those stock prices (and the NASDAQ index that featured them) had developed a speculative bubble.

The outlook for 2001 was favorable. Abby Joseph-Cohen of Goldman Sachs noted "a belief among investors that a quick end to this expansion isn't likely." Ed Kerschner of Paine Webber predicted that the Standard and Poors 500 stock index would be at 1715 by the end of 2001.[1] A poll of financial executives in October 2000 found that 55 percent were confident of sustained U.S. economic growth over the coming two years.[2] In its survey of economists, *Fortune* predicted a slight slowdown but reported no likelihood of recession. "A consensus forecast from the country's top fifty economists" predicted that the economy would grow at 3.5 percent in 2001. *Fortune* assured investors that "the good news is that the expansion is in no danger of ending anytime soon. . . . Though growth is slowing from an extraordinary pace, it is forecast to remain at historically high levels. . . . Wall Street's top strategists and economists are in agreement: Be prepared for average returns in the stock market of close to 10%."[3] On that October 25, the American dollar reached a fresh all-time high against the euro, the troubled notional currency that most of the European Union had rolled out at the beginning of 1999.

The Overthrow of Law

All that changed dramatically during the following two months. What most of the world perceived as the theft of the presidency by George W. Bush abetted by a Supreme Court that halted counting votes in direct contravention of the letter and spirit of the Constitution undermined the belief in the supremacy of the law. It hardly mattered that a year later, newspaper counts proved that Al Gore had indeed won the Florida vote.[4] Alongside political fraud, business

TABLE 5.1.
Comparative Shares of the World Economy, 1999–2011

	USA	*China*	*Japan*	*Germany*	*India*	*France*	*UK*	*Russia*	*Dom*	*Hegem*
1999	22.92%	7.91%	7.41%	4.84%	4.50%	3.62%	3.61%	2.32%	2.90	113.69
2000	22.77%	8.22%	7.23%	4.78%	4.48%	3.58%	3.57%	2.43%	2.77	112.56
2001	22.40%	8.86%	7.06%	4.73%	4.61%	3.55%	3.57%	2.49%	2.53	108.47
2002	22.09%	9.64%	6.86%	4.58%	4.63%	3.47%	3.53%	2.53%	2.29	104.54
2003	21.72%	10.64%	6.69%	4.37%	4.82%	3.36%	3.48%	2.60%	2.04	98.06
2004	21.39%	11.15%	6.52%	4.21%	4.93%	3.28%	3.41%	2.65%	1.92	94.65
2005	21.07%	11.75%	6.31%	4.05%	5.15%	3.19%	3.33%	2.69%	1.79	90.78
2006	20.51%	12.56%	6.09%	3.99%	5.35%	3.10%	3.24%	2.76%	1.63	85.46
2007	19.79%	13.57%	5.89%	3.90%	5.54%	3.00%	3.15%	2.84%	1.46	79.16
2008	18.65%	15.58%	5.51%	3.72%	6.10%	2.83%	2.94%	2.80%	1.20	68.59
2009	18.57%	15.84%	5.38%	3.64%	6.22%	2.85%	2.93%	2.69%	1.17	67.67
2010	18.19%	16.60%	5.34%	3.60%	6.42%	2.75%	2.82%	2.66%	1.10	64.14
2011	17.79%	17.42%	5.10%	3.56%	6.62%	2.68%	2.73%	2.66%	1.02	61.05

Source: The Conference Board Total Economy Database 2012.
Note: The two Purchasing Price Parity measurements have grown far apart: one shows China 12 percent ahead of the United States, the other shows it 17 percent behind for 2011. I have decided to split the difference on these measures. See note to table 4.10.

fraud emerged. The most notorious examples were Enron and Worldcom. These frauds were uncovered only because of their spectacular scale and lack of competence. Suspicions grew that this was just the tip of the iceberg. Furthermore, other shady practices were perfectly legal such as estimating quarterly profits to the public and later quietly reporting lower profits to the Internal Revenue Service on a consistent basis. After tracking each other closely from 1995 to mid-1997, the two figures diverged and reached maximum contrast in the second quarter of 2000 as the reported profits exceeded taxed profits by 64 percent. In 2001–2002 (when the scandals broke and scrutiny grew) the estimates and the reports coincided again, but by 2003, reported profits had diverged again from taxed profits, exceeding them by about 40 percent.[5] In 2004, the IRS changed its reporting rules, making comparisons to previous years difficult. In 2004, U.S. public companies reported $554 billion pretax profits to Wall Street, $394 billion to the IRS.[6]

Even worse, an entire shadow banking system developed without any regulation or monitor. Aside from their age-old commercial and investment roles, banks began to create complex derivatives, options, and swaps. The most notorious were collateralized debt obligations (CDOs). Some observers had warned about the danger of CDOs for years. At the dawn of the shadow banking system in 1998, Brooksley Born, head of the Commodity Futures Trading Commission, had urged that they be banned, but Lawrence Summers and others had shouted her down.[7] After 2001, as the amount of CDOs exploded, Edward Gramlich of the Federal Reserve Board of Governors and Sheila Bair (then a Treasury official) issued sharper warnings. Controller of the Currency John D. Hawke Jr. quashed attempts by state regulators to get a handle on CDOs.[8]

The impact of the overthrow of law was clear, especially for European investors. Many pulled their investments out of American stocks and bonds and placed them in other countries. From November 2000 to January 2001, foreigners reduced their holdings of treasuries by $32 billion, the worst three months in the history of the United States. Most of this came from private individuals, not central banks.[9] Table 5.4 shows that in contrast to other sources, Euroland's investment in U.S. Treasury securities remained flat from 2000 to 2007. This was reflected in the decline of European investment in American stocks. From November 1999 through October 2000, European investors bought a net average of $14 billion each month; in the year that followed, this fell to $7.6 billion a month, and from November 2001 through October 2002 a paltry $2.9 billion.[10] By April 2003, this was a cumulative loss of $285 billion in potential investment. Small wonder that the American stock market crashed and has never (in real terms) regained the levels of 2000. This was misleadingly conflated as the "bursting of the tech bubble," although one can find many major companies unrelated to technology, telecommunications, or dot-com companies whose stocks lost over half their value in this time.[11] Even when the S&P 500 recovered from 2003 to 2007, its growth lagged behind every other country's stock index, with the exceptions of Trinidad, Jamaica, Ecuador, and Costa Rica.[12] With the wind in its sails, the actual euro currency debuted in January 2002. Countries that had shied away from euro-denominated bonds now snapped them up and the euro seemed destined to be a coequal reserve currency.

From October 25, 2000, to January 5, 2001, the dollar lost 13 percent of its value against the euro. Almost half of that came in the ten trading days following the Supreme Court's announcement. Other currencies were not as affected, and despite the pullout of European money, the dollar index rose to a new high against a basket of the U.S. trading partners during the winter of 2001–2002 as war and uncertainty helped drive money towards the greenback. From February 27, 2002, to July 16, 2008, the overall dollar index fell 20 percent against its trading partners. The Federal Reserve's dollar index against major traded currencies had peaked in March 1985 at 143.9. In March

TABLE 5.2.
Net Foreign Direct Investment in the United States, 1997–2011 (in billion $)

	Amount Table 3_10, line 34	*Change*	*Net Foreign purchase of stocks Table 3_24, line 3*	*S & P 500 change*
1997	106.000			
1998	179.000	68.87%		27.10%
1999	289.000	61.45%		19.50%
2000	321.274	11.17%		-10.10%
2001	151.581	-52.82%	116.39	-13.00%
2002	80.841	-46.67%	50.19	-23.40%
2003	67.090	-17.01%	34.74	26.40%
2004	145.812	117.34%	28.48	9.00%
2005	112.638	-22.75%	81.99	3.00%
2006	241.961	114.81%	150.42	13.60%
2007	237.542	-1.83%	195.52	3.53%
2008	310.961	30.91%	44.80	-38.49%
2009	158.581	-49.00%	152.73	19.67%
2010	236.226	48.96%	109.74	11.00%
2011	227.866	-3.54%	25.08	-1.12%

Source: Federal Reserve Bulletin, Statistical Supplement, posted 1998–May 2012, accessed June 3, 2012, www.federalreserve.gov/pubs/supplement/2008/12/table3_24pl.htm and www.federalreserve.gov/pubs/supplement/2004/01/table3_24 and table 3_10.

2008, the dollar hit an all-time low in that index at 70.35. The dollar had lost 51 percent of its value since 1985 and 48 percent of its value against the euro since 2000.[13] Asian investors, most importantly Japan and China with their own crony systems, were not much troubled by the scandals. Money from Japan and China balanced the trade deficit. The Bank of Japan invested in dollars in order to keep the yen low while other Japanese investors engaged in the "carry trade," borrowing at very low domestic interest rates and investing in higher-yielding securities, including U.S. bonds, notes, and bills. In May 2006, the OECD warned that "most observers agree that eventually a current account rebalancing looks unavoidable, that the correction will involve an adjustment in the trade balance and that the dollar depreciation needed to achieve this could be large (of the order of one-third to one-half)."[14] From April 2006 to mid-July 2008, the dollar lost 26 percent of its value against the Australian dollar, 25 percent against the Brazilian real, 13 percent against the British pound, 14 percent against the Canadian dollar, 15 percent against the Chinese yuan, 23 percent against the euro, 10 percent against the Japanese yen, 12 percent against the Malaysian ringgit, 16 percent against the Singapore dollar, 22 percent against the Swiss franc, and 13 percent against the Thai baht. The overall value of the dollar against the currencies of its major trade partners fell 12.1 percent. The financial crisis of 2008 changed the balance dramatically when many took refuge in the dollar. In 2009 the dollar's "Bush penalty" against the euro ended.

The Problems of U.S. Bond Sales

Compounding this problem was a new budget deficit. The Republicans were determined to restore the budget deficits to the Reagan/Bush days by cutting taxes on the richest Americans. Revenue shared with the states was cut so those states would have to raise their taxes, generally sales taxes and property taxes. Rules were changed so that the surplus revenue received in the trust funds (particularly the pension portion of Social Security) could offset deficits. The practice continued of having the Social Security trust funds and other governmental entities buy up to half of the federal debt. This however was different than earlier times because most projections suggested that the surplus flows into Social Security would end around 2017. At that point, the funds would have to market increasing portions of their securities to the public. From October 2000 to October 2007, the federal government issued $3,322.04 billion in debt. Of the total, 51.07 percent was taken by the federal government itself, 8.07 percent by the Federal Reserve, and $1,357.39 billion (40.86 percent) by the public. This changed with the financial crisis. The Federal Reserve's share of the debt returned to levels not seen since the 1970s, but the Fed's "quantitative easing" was balanced by the massive destruction of private credit. That explains why inflation and interest rates have remained low.

It needs to be understood that the "public" in this last figure does not particularly refer to the American public. The central banks of Japan and China

TABLE 5.3.
Development of National Debt, 1960–2012

End FY	*As % GDP*	*% held by government*	*% held by U.S. public*	*% held by Federal Reserve*	*% foreign-held*
1960	55.99%	18.49%	72.39%	9.12%	(NA)
1965	46.88%	19.08%	64.97%	12.13%	3.81%
1970	37.61%	25.65%	55.53%	15.15%	3.15%
1975	34.73%	27.16%	44.97%	15.69%	12.18%
1980	33.37%	21.68%	51.64%	13.29%	13.39%
1985	43.83%	17.07%	61.33%	9.34%	12.26%
1990	55.91%	24.79%	54.17%	7.31%	13.73%
1995	67.03%	26.75%	49.38%	7.60%	16.27%
1996	67.13%	27.93%	45.65%	7.54%	18.88%
1997	65.38%	29.74%	39.66%	7.91%	22.69%
1998	63.24%	32.07%	37.35%	8.36%	22.21%
1999	60.87%	35.20%	33.07%	8.86%	22.87%
2000	57.31%	39.42%	32.70%	9.09%	18.79%
2001	56.43%	42.47%	30.85%	9.26%	17.43%
2002	58.79%	42.88%	27.16%	10.58%	19.37%
2003	61.57%	42.11%	26.68%	9.71%	21.51%
2004	62.99%	41.59%	24.43%	9.52%	24.46%
2005	63.60%	41.91%	24.35%	10.08%	24.41%
2006	63.99%	42.86%	24.05%	9.10%	23.96%
2007	64.58%	43.75%	22.55%	8.71%	24.97%
2008	69.67%	41.89%	25.16%	4.92%	28.06%
2009	85.20%	36.47%	26.95%	6.48%	30.07%
2010	94.21%	33.34%	28.70%	6.00%	31.96%
2011	98.70%	31.40%	25.76%	11.28%	31.56%
2012[a]	104.80%	29.19%			

Sources: White House, Office of Management and Budget, The Budget for Fiscal Year 2009, Historical Tables, 132–133, 195, Analytical Perspectives, 244. Budget for Fiscal Year 2007, Analytical Perspectives, 233–234. The Budget for Fiscal Year 2011, Historical Tables, 133–34; Analytical Perspectives, 69, The Budget for Fiscal Year 2012, Historical Tables, 140. The Budget for Fiscal Year 2013, Historical Tables, 140; Analytical Perspectives, 82.

Note: [a] estimate

purchased a large portion of that $1,357 billion. Foreign presence at auctions hovered at the 40 percent range. From 1998 to 2001, the public holdings of debt declined as the budget was in surplus. The data from the White House OMB state that in 2002 the Treasury Department increased the net public debt by $221 billion of which foreigners bought 88.4 percent; in 2003 foreigners bought 67.94 percent of the $373 billion net increase in public debt; in 2004 foreigners bought 90.2 percent of the $382.1 billion net increase in public debt. In 2005, foreigners bought 44.5 percent of $296.7 billion. In 2006, they bought an estimated 85.7 percent of $236.8 billion, then the figure was revised to 40.8 percent. For 2007, the figures suggest that foreigners bought over 100 percent ($209 billion of the $206.2 billion net increase) which suggests some problems in comparing treasury figures. By 2008, foreigners held 48 percent of tradeable U.S. debt.[15] The Treasury Department uses somewhat different measurements; by its figures foreign ownership of marketable debt rose from 35 percent in the first quarter of 2000 to 51 percent in the first quarter of 2005 and stabilized at that level.[16] The pattern of foreign ownership of U.S. debt also changed markedly as table 5.4 demonstrates. Japan, China, the Caribbean bank centers, and the oil exporters bought most of the note and bond issues from 2000 to 2007. In particular the central banks of China and Japan own a large amount of U.S. government debt and could dump it if they wanted to.

In the late 1990s bill and bond auctions were very popular when the government was buying back debt. After 2001, the demand at auctions slumped noticeably. From October 2001 to November 2007, only one long-term bond auction was above average, meaning demand exceeded supply by 2.17 times. The Treasury Department's web site lists 986 auctions of two- to ten-year notes from 1980 to 2010.[17] The average demand is about 2.3 times the supply. Since 1980, here are the stretches exceeding three months where demand has been continuously below average:

1. May 2002–September 2003	17 months
2. January–October 1999	9 months
2. October 2007–June 2008	9 months
4. June 1998–January 1999	7 months
5. January–July 2000	6 months
6. March–August 2001	5 months
7. September 2003–January 2004	4 months
7. November 2000–March 2001	4 months
7. January 2002–May 2002	4 months
7. September 1982–January 1983	4 months
7. February–June 1982	4 months

TABLE 5.4.
Comparison of Foreign Holdings of U.S. Government Securities, 2000–2011 (in billion $)

	October 2000	*October 2007*	*Change*	*October 2011*	*Change*
GRAND TOTAL	1035.2	2299.2	122.10%	4908.3	113.48%
by selected nation:					
China	59.5	467.7	686.05%	1256.0	168.55%
Japan	317.7	601.7	89.39%	1006.8	67.33%
Belgium-Luxemburg	23.4	77.9	232.91%	258.8	232.22%
Oil Exporters	48	141.6	195.00%	245.6	73.45%
Brazil	<10.9	113.9		229.4	101.40%
Caribbean bank centers	39.2	105.6	169.39%	212.0	100.76%
"All other"	158.3	162	2.34%	197.9	22.16%
Taiwan	34.4	40.7	18.31%	167.5	311.55%
Russia	<8.5	33.6		147.5	338.99%
Switzerland	17.4	37.8	117.24%	143.9	280.69%
Hong Kong	38.7	51.3	32.56%	113.3	120.86%
UK[a]	60.4	120.3	99.17%	106.8	-11.22%
South Korea	28.3	37	30.74%	42.7	15.41%
Foreign government/ bank holdings	615.1	1613.8	162.36%	3597.8	122.94%
of which:					
Treasury bills	155.1	180.4	16.31%	374.6	107.65%
Treasury notes/bonds	460	1433.4	211.61%	3223.2	124.86%

Source: www.treasury.gov/resource-center/data-chart-center/tic/Documents/mfhhos01.txt, accessed June 3, 2012; Daniel Kruger, "Oil Brings Americans Closer to OPEC Debtor Dependence," Bloomberg News, July 14, 2008, accessed September 13, 2008.

Note: [a] Some suggest that Middle Eastern oil producers make some of their security purchases through the United Kingdom.

The above-average auction in September 2003 was the only break in a streak of twenty-one months. Of the eleven longest streaks, six occurred between Election Day 2000 and the deepening of the financial crisis in 2008. The crisis brought a flight to safety and since the summer of 2008, U.S. auctions regularly enjoy up to three times demand over supply.

Future Indicators: Health, Power, Transport, Education

The indicators of future prosperity and continued U.S. dominance are not good. First, let us review the latest vital statistics.[18]

The female life expectancy at birth in 2009 was:

1. Japan	86.4
2. Singapore	85.8
3. Spain	84.9
4. Switzerland	84.6
5. France	84.4
6. Canada	84.3
7. Australia	83.9
8. Finland	83.5
8. Italy	83.5
8. Israel	83.5
11. Sweden	83.4
12. Iceland	83.3
12. Luxemburg	83.3
14. Norway	83.2
14. Austria	83.2
16. Belgium	82.8
16. South Korea	82.8
16. Germany	82.8
19. Greece	82.7
19. New Zealand	82.7
19. Netherlands	82.7
22. Portugal	82.6
23. Ireland	82.5
23. United Kingdom	82.5
25. Jordan	81.5
26. Taiwan	81.4
27. Slovenia	81.2
28. Denmark	81.1
29. Chile	80.9
30. United States, White	80.8
30. Georgia	80.8
32. Cyprus	80.7
32. Czech Republic	80.7
32. Panama	80.7
35. Costa Rica	80.5
35. Lithuania	80.5
37. United States, All	80.4
37. Argentina	80.4
39. Poland	80.3

39. Albania	80.3
41. Cuba	80.1

The infant mortality per 1,000 live births in 2009 was:

1. Japan	2.3
2. Singapore	2.7
2. Sweden	2.7
4. Iceland	3.2
5. France	3.3
6. Spain	3.4
6. Finland	3.4
8. Norway	3.5
8. Germany	3.5
10. Malta	3.7
10. Czech Republic	3.7
12. Netherlands	3.8
13. Ireland	3.9
14. Switzerland	4.1
14. Israel	4.1
16. Slovenia	4.2
16. South Korea	4.2
16. Denmark	4.2
19. Austria	4.3
19. Belgium	4.3
21. Luxemburg	4.4
22. Australia	4.6
22. United Kingdom	4.6
24. Portugal	4.7
25. New Zealand	4.8
26. Canada	4.9
26. Cuba	4.9
28. Greece	5.0
29. United States, White	5.1
30. Taiwan	5.2
31. Hungary	5.3
32. Italy	5.4
33. United States, All	6.1
34. Croatia	6.2
35. Lithuania	6.3
36. Poland	6.5

37. Slovakia	6.6
38. Estonia	7.1
39. Chile	7.3
40. Kuwait	8.1
41. Latvia	8.4

From a once-commanding position, the United States has fallen to thirty-third in infant mortality and thirty-seventh in female life expectancy. Even the white numbers have fallen out of the top twenty. There is a similar issue with American height. John Komlos and Benjamin Lauderdale in the *Social Science Quarterly* found that Americans are now shorter than Western and Northern Europeans. The stagnation of American heights is clear even if you restrict comparison to native-born non-Hispanic whites.[19] There is a general sense that the United States is a much poorer nation than its per capita GDP would indicate even using the least favorable estimates of table 1.3. It also shows how far behind in absolute terms the United States has fallen. The United States is as far behind Japan in health as Jamaica is behind the United States. In health terms, the United States is not in the top rank of wealthy nations. The closest nations are Albania, Cyprus, Costa Rica, Panama, Argentina, Lithuania, Poland, Cuba, and the Czech Republic for life expectancy. The closest nations are Greece, Italy, Cuba, Taiwan, Hungary, Croatia, Lithuania, Poland, Estonia, and Slovakia for infant mortality. The average per capita GDP of these nations is $21,346. The United States claims a per capita GDP of $48,000. This suggests a potential for a 56 percent adjustment in American purchasing values from 2011. In 2007, it was 61 percent, suggesting that an adjustment is under way. Because of its large military budget and the need to maintain the overseas empire, there is a substantial difference between per capita income and per capita GDP in the United States as shown in table 5.9.

Education is harder to measure. The international tests mainly cover math and science in a small group of developed countries.[20] In no test has the United States ranked first or second. Perhaps most telling is a poll concerning belief in evolution in thirty-two European countries plus Japan and the United States. Only about half of Americans polled believed that humans had evolved from earlier species. This was thirty-third out of the thirty-four countries. Turkey ranked lowest. Iceland led with 85 percent. The ratio of acceptance to nonacceptance had changed from 45–48 in 1985 to 40–39, with a whopping 21 percent saying they did not know.[21] The proficiency of American students in reading, writing, mathematics, and science did not change appreciably from 1976 to 1998.[22] Among OECD nations in a 1989 survey, the United States had the highest percentage of people aged twenty-five to sixty-four who had completed high school but was fourth behind Germany, Japan, and Switzerland among those aged twenty-five to thirty-four.[23] The American high school graduation rate did not rise from 1970 to 2004.[24] The percentage of students enrolled in foreign language classes rose, but almost all of the increase was in Spanish.[25] The percentage of high school graduates who enrolled in college within twelve months peaked in 1997 then declined slightly.[26] The 2004 surveys saw further deterioration of American education. For the population aged twenty-five to sixty-four, the United States was now second in attainment of secondary education and fourth in years of education, and fifth in completion of postsecondary education. Within the cohort aged twenty-five to thirty-four, the United States ranked eleventh in each category. In the 2009 update, the American twenty-five to thirty-four cohort ranked eleventh in attaining secondary education and fifteenth in attaining postsecondary education.[27] This provides statistical support to the argument that the United States is falling behind the rest of world in education.

In 2003, U.S. research and development led the world with $291.9 billion, about 34 percent of the world total; Japan had about 16 percent of the world total. On basic research as a percentage of research and development, the United States ranked eleventh; on nonmilitary research as a percentage of the economy, it ranked twenty-second.[28]

Mass transit ridership declined 80 percent despite the postwar sprawl. In 1946, the population in the United States was about 140 million people, who took 23 billion mass transit rides. This works out to 167 rides per person. By the year 1957, the U.S. population had grown, but rides dropped to sixty per person. While the population continued to grow, the ratio of mass transit rides continued to drop reaching its lowest point in 1972 at 31.24. There was no rebound until 2008, when the ratio reached 35.31.[29]

Increasingly, transport relied on the truck and the automobile. This in turn depended on cheap gasoline. The rise in the cost of gasoline after 1997 drove some to mass transit and deprived others of mobility entirely. The total miles driven by Americans peaked in November 2007 at 3.039 trillion and stood at 2.96 trillion in November 2011.[30] But this does not give the full picture. If we account for the growth of population and so look at the per capita miles driven, the effect is starker. The peak here is June 2005 and we have steadily fallen back to the level of January 1997, a 7 percent drop.[31] This relates to the housing crisis because of tighter credit, but also because families had bought houses that were long drives from their jobs and their shopping. High gasoline prices made this lifestyle unsustainable for some. The worst-hit areas in this crisis have been suburbs and even more the so-called exurbs. As developments emptied out, their very emptiness deterred potential buyers and accelerated their slide into "shruburbs" haunted by squatters and thieves stripping houses of valuable pipes and wires. The California counties with the highest foreclosure rates are those that had become exurbs of San Francisco and Los Angeles.[32] In 2011, population grew more in Bronx County than Nassau County, New York.[33] When is the last time that happened?

The drop in vehicle-miles driven per capita is even starker if we just look at sixteen- to thirty-four-year-olds. Since 2001, their per capita vehicle miles driven are down 23 percent. The same group has increased its passenger miles on public transit by 40 percent.[34] This reflects not only the high price of gas, but also the relative unavailability of cheap used cars. Historically, the average age of an active American vehicle was eight years. Recently, it has risen to over ten years.[35] When people could not afford new cars and retained their older cars, it broke the chain that allowed eighteen- to twenty-five-year-olds to buy starter cars.

Productivity Woes

With these problems in health and education and transportation, it is no surprise that per-hour productivity continued to have problems. Despite the falling dollar, the trade deficit got steadily worse and American exports became steadily less competitive. In 2004, Germany again passed the United States in international volume of exports. From 2004 to 2006, China's exports as a percentage of the leading nation's exports rose from 65 percent to 87 percent. The United States fell to third place in 2007, despite the

TABLE 5.5.
World Merchandise Exports by Nation, 2011, a.k.a. "Most Competitive Nation in the World"

	millions$	*Index (China=100)*
China	1,899	100.00
United States	1,481	77.99
Germany	1,474	77.62
Japan	823	43.34
Netherlands	660	34.76
France	597	31.44
South Korea	555	29.23
Italy	523	27.54
Russia	522	27.49
Belgium	476	25.07

Source: www.wto.org/english/news_e/pres12_e/pr658_e.htm, posted April 12, 2012, accessed June 5, 2012.

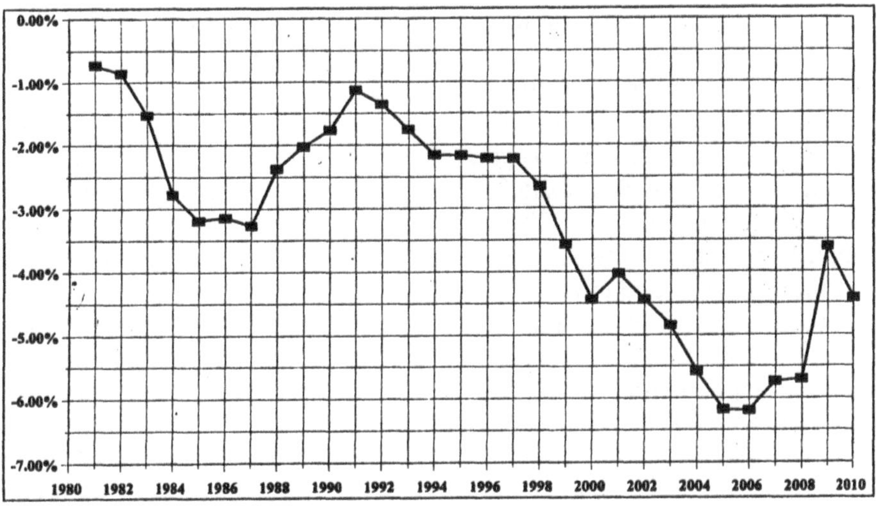

Figure 5.2 U.S. Trade Deficit as Percentage of GDP

euro's appreciation. In 2009, China took over the lead in world exports. The United States caught up to Germany again in 2011.

The trade deficit as a percentage of U.S. GDP grew alarmingly before the financial crisis. Since the deficit is deducted from GDP, it not only takes away from the American store of assets, it also depresses GDP growth for the year. The worsening position as seen in figure 5.2 from 1993 to 2000 came from economic improvement (which increases imports) and the residual effects of the Reagan/Bush deficits. Leveling off starting in 2006 could be anticipated from the creation of a surplus under Clinton. From 2007 to 2011 there would be a tendency for the trade deficit to improve. The data did fall as predicted, but they are complicated by economic downturn and the decline in oil imports.

Imperial Overstretch

Further problems came from American imperial overstretch. The prolonged wars in Afghanistan and Iraq and a general spending spree for unnecessary weapons systems caused the military budget to move up. The percentage of the economy devoted to the official military budget bottomed out at 2.81 percent in 1999. It rose steadily to 3.98 percent by 2005. At least another 1 percent of GDP has been dedicated to the wars. Starting in 2007, this took an ongoing 0.5 percent away from GDP. By 2012, the GDP was 2.5 percent or more lower than it would have been otherwise.[36]

The recent wars demonstrate the problems of overstretch as shown by Kennedy. It is worth looking back at the Iraq conflict, even though most U.S. troops have left under the Status of Forces Agreement (SOFA). At first glance, Iraq should have been a negligible war. If we return to the Introduction's formula for military potential strength, Iraq gets 8.7 for GDP, 1.7 for population, 8.8 for per capita GDP, and 2.6 for expanse, for a total of 21.7 as opposed to the United States at 277.17. The first part of the war went very quickly and toppled the Saddam Hussein government. Then an insurgency developed. The army's current counterinsurgency doctrine states "most density recommendations fall within a range of twenty to twenty-five counterinsurgents for every 1,000 inhabitants of an AO (area of occupation)."[37] Assuming 23 million people in Iraq, it requires 2 percent of that total, that is, 460,000 counterinsurgents including combat troops, Iraqi military, and police. As of 2006, there were 670,000 active duty U.S. army soldiers and marines.[38] There were an additional 150,000 members of the U.S. Army National Guard and Reserve. Only a fraction of these are combat troops. An army and marine corps of 1.4 million would bring them up to Vietnam levels. In 1970, the army and marine corps numbered 1.583 million.[39] All of this is very costly: these troops must be recruited (or drafted), trained, and equipped. These soldiers must be housed, transported, and kept healthy. An increase in the military budget would lower the GDP and then would come the issue of paying for it: a tax increase of this magnitude would be politically unthinkable and ruinous to the economy. Overall productivity would be hurt by taking out 10 percent of the male population aged 18 to 24.[40]

The low levels of American education led to constant misunderstandings and confrontations. Bush's signing of the SOFA and a generous payment to the Sunnis of central Iraq brought a recession of violence. It did not follow the recommendations in the Counterinsurgency Manual and was not a vindication of the "coin" strategy. Some however, thought it was and tried a similar approach to Afghanistan with little success. Modern wars can be won, but the cost in blood and treasure is terrible to pay.

The Flight of U.S. Assets

The changing position of the United States in the world has slowly and subtly reshaped investment and corporate profit. It has been widely noted that many "American" corporations now draw greater profits from abroad and have ever less interest in building new facilities in the United States or hiring Americans or providing philanthropy to their communities. Stock investments have shown a similar change. Before 2003, the value of foreign stocks owned by U.S. citizens was comparable to the value of U.S. stocks owned by foreign citizens. Table 5.6 shows that the lagging of U.S. stock values has created a noticeable gap and that there is a strong desire by Americans to invest in foreign stocks. It uses the main London stock index, the FTSE, as a proxy for market value to give us a sense of investment and disinvestment separate from the level of price changes. We are using the dollar value of the FTSE so as to account for the change in the British pound's value. On both sides of the equation, investment each year has exceeded the mere change in the value of the exchange, but there has been more American investment in foreign exchanges than foreign investment in U.S. markets. Small wonder that the American market underperformed compared to most of the world's markets.

The Rise of Asia and Europe

In the concluding chapter of *The Rise and Fall of the Great Powers*, Paul Kennedy predicted that by 2000, the world percentage of GDP produced by Asia would "very likely" exceed 20 percent.[41] In fact, China and Japan by themselves held 19.5 percent. Asia's share exceeded 30 percent.

In considering Europe, Kennedy suggested that the position of Western Europe depended on its ability to achieve greater coordination through the (then) EEC. Three unexpected events have worked greatly to Europe's advantage: the revolutions of 1989, the subsequent Soviet collapse, and the collapse

TABLE 5.6.
Change in Stock Ownership, 2002–2010

	Foreign stocks owned by Americans (in billions)	*Change*	*Change in $ value of FTSE*	*U.S. stocks owned by foreigners (in billions)*	*Change*	*Change in value S&P 500*
2002	$1,373.98			$1,248.09		
2003	$2,079.42	51.34%	24.64%	$1,712.07	37.18%	26.40%
2004	$2,560.42	23.13%	14.07%	$1,960.36	14.50%	9.00%
2005	$3,317.70	29.58%	5.41%	$2,109.86	7.63%	3.00%
2006	$4,328.96	30.48%	22.88%	$2,547.47	20.74%	13.60%
2007	$5,247.99	21.23%	3.51%	$2,900.95	13.88%	3.53%
2008	$2,748.42	-47.63%	-49.44%	$1,850.06	-36.23%	-38.49%
2009	$3,945.30	43.55%	29.80%	$2,494.28	34.82%	19.67%
2010[a]	$4,485.59	13.69%	3.98%	$2,991.63	19.94%	11.00%

Source: U.S. Bureau of Economic Analysis, accessed June 3, 2012, www.bea.gov/international/xls/intinv10_t2.xls.
Note: [a] Preliminary

of the dollar after 2000. These have smoothed over what might have been an impossible transition to the euro and greater economic management. They greatly expanded the area and population of "Europe." Western European growth was sacrificed in order to make areas stretching to the Urals more productive. Much of this was extremely painful as factories that had employed thousands were closed. Unemployment in the former Warsaw Pact areas remains very high. Table 5.7 shows a real unemployment rate by taking the maximum percentage of population employed as a benchmark and then calculating a percentage of that maximum. This balances cultural factors and traditions such as the employment of women, the young, and the old.

China may seem to be the most immediate challenge, but the European Union and Russia also loom. The EU spent the ten years after the 1989 revolutions trying to rebuild the east. Since 1999, it has focused on increasing the Union's integration, symbolized by the rise of the single currency and the European Central Bank. Some American publications including the *New York Times* predicted confusion. "Will chaos reign when much of Europe starts changing over to euro coins and notes? Will lines clog the aisles of supermarkets as cashiers fumble trying to figure out euro change? Will citizens hoard their new euro coins as collectors' items? Will people feel so ill at ease with the new prices that they just won't buy anything beyond the basics?"[42] The answers to all these questions was a resounding no. Within a couple of weeks local currencies had been swept from circulation, although prices were being quoted in both currencies and cash registers were showing both prices as long as the old currency was being accepted.

More predictable was the fate of Stability and Growth Pact, which set the limits of budget deficits and debts. When they were waived to allow entrance of Italy and Greece into the Eurozone, their "flexibility" was demonstrated, as the commissioners used the fig-leaf excuse of "making progress." In July 2002, the European Commission found that Portugal was in violation of the budget guidelines; the Portuguese promised to do better. Germany also appeared likely to breach the limit. In October, however, the European Commission ordered France to cut its deficit, and France refused. Romano Prodi, then the chair of the European Commission, called the Stability Pact guidelines "stupid." The Italian government avoided reprimand by using accounting gimmicks that would make Arthur Andersen and Enron blush. The *New York Times* chided "a scofflaw in Rome, a mutiny in Paris, and a pair of admitted perpetrators in Berlin and Lisbon."[43] But this missed the point, as do most American analyses of European economies. The limits always were silly, as if we would consider throwing Alaska out of the U.S. dollar zone for carrying a per capita public debt that is three times the national average. The alternative is to use contractionary fiscal policy in time of economic down-

TABLE 5.7.
Comparison of Real Unemployment (percentage of population employed as percentage of peak)

	Canada	*Czech*	*France*	*Germany*	*Hungary*	*Italy*	*Japan*	*Poland*	*Switz*	*UK*	*USA*
1992	5.76%	7.03%	4.27%	2.06%	19.85%	0.66%	0.00%	19.23%	2.60%	5.60%	2.65%
1993	6.59%	7.28%	5.97%	3.83%	25.24%	3.45%	0.06%	20.96%	4.26%	6.70%	2.36%
1994	5.75%	6.31%	6.23%	4.74%	27.41%	5.14%	0.29%	21.61%	5.66%	5.05%	1.17%
1995	5.27%	5.58%	5.80%	4.96%	27.96%	5.40%	0.49%	21.05%	6.22%	5.38%	0.75%
1996	5.54%	4.60%	5.83%	5.61%	27.74%	4.96%	0.29%	20.16%	6.63%	4.78%	0.36%
1997	4.45%	4.32%	5.79%	6.09%	27.60%	4.78%	0.00%	19.08%	6.78%	3.35%	0.00%
1998	3.10%	5.70%	4.76%	4.64%	26.11%	3.90%	1.41%	18.17%	5.64%	2.73%	0.00%
1999	1.60%	8.84%	3.26%	4.75%	23.80%	2.93%	2.99%	21.38%	5.22%	1.83%	0.00%
2000	0.15%	8.92%	1.14%	4.37%	22.95%	1.28%	3.79%	22.60%	5.01%	1.06%	0.00%
2001	0.00%	8.42%	0.00%	4.17%	23.15%	0.00%	4.77%	24.29%	4.45%	0.56%	0.85%
2002	0.00%	7.85%	0.00%	5.13%	23.16%	0.00%	6.45%	26.55%	3.49%	0.11%	2.03%
2003	0.00%	9.06%	0.13%	6.25%	22.95%	0.00%	6.89%	27.36%	3.75%	0.00%	2.46%
2004	0.00%	8.70%	0.57%	5.59%	23.92%	0.00%	6.79%	26.42%	4.78%	0.00%	2.29%
2005	0.00%	7.70%	0.78%	5.44%	23.99%	0.00%	6.45%	24.77%	4.86%	0.00%	1.48%
2006	0.00%	5.87%	1.09%	0.00%	23.42%	0.00%	6.05%	22.29%	3.16%	0.90%	0.00%
2007	0.00%	5.00%	0.00%	0.00%	23.57%	0.00%	5.74%	18.61%	1.87%	0.67%	0.00%
2008	0.00%	2.72%	0.08%	0.00%	24.43%	0.50%	6.08%	15.50%	0.00%	0.00%	1.36%
2009	2.40%	3.82%	1.79%	0.00%	26.49%	2.74%	7.53%	15.19%	0.00%	2.13%	5.85%
2010	1.89%	5.33%	2.16%	0.00%	26.23%	3.91%	8.37%	14.72%	0.00%	2.47%	6.77%
2011	1.12%	4.51%	2.08%	0.00%	25.28%	4.08%	8.47%	13.82%	0.00%	2.17%	7.09%

Source: Derived from The Conference Board Total Economy Database, 2012.
Note: This measure counts each new peak of percentage of population employed as full employment (0 percent). It is measured against subsequent percentages of population employed. This avoids the problems of different measures used by each country and changing methods by government offices. It gives us a consistent and comparable measurement.

turn, the very same policies that led German voters to support Adolf Hitler. Prodi was absolutely right, and the sooner such limits are laughed off, the better. The European Central Bank's demands for strict fiscal policy have been matched by tight monetary policy. Despite the sluggish economy, the bank kept its benchmark rate high.[44] When the crunch came in 2008, the dollar outperformed the euro. In 2007, France, Germany, Ireland, Italy, Portugal, and Spain all had full employment. Ireland and Spain had surplus budgets. Ireland and Iceland, like the United States, saw massive layoffs in 2008 from the crisis of the shadow banking system. Iceland terminated the crisis by allowing the banks to fail. Ireland caused a fiscal crisis by writing a blank check to the banks. The second stage shows the devastation caused by foolish austerity policies in Greece, Spain, and Ireland (again). In the current European crisis, some writers suggest that leaving the euro would make countries more competitive. However, the market could determine the value of a resurrected drachma or peseta in unpredictable ways. A move out of the euro might cause economic turmoil without making a country's goods more competitive on the international market. Germany, reaching new highs of employment for the last several years, must shoulder the burden of leadership and aid its brothers in the spirit of the Rome Treaty of 1957. The current packages of financial aid are not going to the distressed countries but straight back to the German banks and the ECB.[45] Far more useful and ingratiating would be direct aid, whether it is paying Siemens to modernize the Greek railroad system or providing free Greek vacations to some lucky German families.

The Bagehot Maneuver after 2004

Sluggish growth in U.S. real per capita income worsened persistent unemployment from 2001 to 2005. Even when the U.S. economy reached full employment in 2006, and a higher percentage of the population was working then ever before, many were living on the margins where a single emergency could push them over the edge.

The 2004 election caused more damage to the American economy. As a member of the Organization for Security and Cooperation in Europe (OSCE), the United States is obliged to invite international experts to observe its elections. Before the 2000 debacle, the OSCE had never bothered. In 2002, it sent monitors for the mid-term elections, mainly to the state of Florida.[46] In 2004, its Office of Democratic Institutions and Human Rights sent ninety-two observers led by Rita Süssmuth of Germany and Barbara Hering of Switzerland.[48] The mission got off to a bad start as Colorado barred the observers entirely, and Florida forbade them from observing the polling places.[49]

TABLE 5.8.
Comparison of Real Unemployment: Selected European Countries since the Crisis
(percentage of population employed as percentage of peak)

	Czech	*France*	*Germany*	*Hungary*	*Ireland*	*Italy*	*Portugal*	*Spain*	*Poland*	*Switz*	*UK*
2007	5.00%	0.00%	0.00%	23.57%	0.00%	0.00%	0.00%	0.00%	18.61%	1.87%	0.67%
2008	2.72%	0.08%	0.00%	24.43%	3.23%	0.50%	0.00%	1.69%	15.50%	0.00%	0.00%
2009	3.82%	1.79%	0.00%	26.49%	12.31%	2.74%	2.87%	9.03%	15.19%	0.00%	2.13%
2010	5.33%	2.16%	0.00%	26.23%	16.77%	3.91%	4.61%	11.80%	14.72%	0.00%	2.47%
2011	4.51%	2.08%	0.00%	25.28%	19.19%	4.08%	5.83%	13.09%	13.82%	0.00%	2.17%

Source: The Conference Board Total Economy Database 2012.
Note: This measure counts each new peak of percentage of population employed as full employment (0 percent). It is measured against subsequent percentages of population employed. This avoids the problems of different measures used by each country and changing methods by government offices. It gives us a consistent and comparable measurement.

TABLE 5.9.
U.S. Economic Performance, 2000–2009

Year	Per capita GDP	Real Change	Per capita Disposable Income	Real Change	Consumer Price Index
2000	35,237		25,944		3.40%
2001	36,049	-0.50%	26,805	0.52%	2.80%
2002	36,935	0.86%	27,799	2.11%	1.60%
2003	38,310	1.42%	28,805	1.32%	2.30%
2004	40,435	2.85%	30,287	2.44%	2.70%
2005	42,664	2.11%	31,318	0.00%	3.40%
2006	44,805	1.82%	33,157	2.67%	3.20%
2007	46,611	1.23%	34,445	1.08%	2.80%
2008	47,375	-2.16%	35,450	-0.88%	3.80%
2009	46,364	-1.73%	35,526	0.61%	-0.40%

Sources: Commerce Department, Bureau of Economic Analysis; Labor Department, Bureau of Labor Statistics, revisions as of June 3, 2012.

Widespread fraud including major discrepancies in twenty-one states between exit poll results and announced results marred the elections. All of these discrepancies favored Bush. The exit polls had Kerry winning the popular and electoral vote including the states of Ohio and New Mexico, and perhaps Iowa, Nevada, and Florida. There were also wide discrepancies in non-swing states. In Pennsylvania, for example, the exit poll as of 12:21 a.m. with 1,930 respondents showed that Kerry would get between 53.7 percent and 54.6 percent of the state's vote. The official reports had Kerry winning 50.9 percent of the vote, a discrepancy of at least 2.8 percent to 3.7 percent outside the margin of error. A new exit poll was put up at 2:06 p.m. adding 177 more respondents, 78 percent of whom favored Bush to bring the polls in line with the official results. In the decisive state of Ohio, there was a discrepancy of at least 2.9 percent which swung the electoral college to Bush.[50] The OSCE drily referred to "some divergences that appeared to be mostly within the exit polls' margins of error."[51] The monitors were allowed into eleven states, but "access was sometimes limited to specific counties or to specific polling stations within a particular county, contrary to OSCE commitments."[52] In newspaper reports, the observers stated that they had less access to the polls than in Kazakhstan, that Venezuela's electronic voting system was more fraud-proof, and that the ballots were more complex than any the observers had seen, including those of the Republic of Georgia.[53]

The 2004 election controversy raised the specter of another big drop in the dollar and consequent inflation. The dollar lost 5 percent of its value from Election Day 2004 to the Federal Reserve's Open Market Committee meeting of December 14, 2004. "A number of participants cited the depreciation of the dollar on foreign markets [et al.] as factors tending to boost the upside risks to their inflation outlook. . . . The depreciation of the dollar had been notable."[54] The committee quietly worked out a maneuver that invoked "Bagehot's Rule." The nineteenth-century editor of *The Economist* had written that "very large loans at very high rates are the best remedy for the worst malady of the money market when a foreign drain is added to a domestic drain."[55] To keep foreign funds in the United States and encourage new foreign investment, the interest rate was hiked. This was not part of a general tightening of credit because the money supply was loosened correspondingly. In November 2004, the year-over-year change in the real seasonally adjusted M3 money supply was 2.2 percent while the real interest rate was 1.37 percent; a year later, as table 5.10 shows, the money supply had grown 3.77 percent in real terms while the real interest rate stood at 3.5 percent. From November 9, 2004, the Federal Reserve raised its funds rate from 1.75 percent up to 5.25 percent by June 2006. The Fed dared not raise the short-term rates any further because housing prices were beginning to fall and the European Central Bank and Bank of England were raising their own rates. The Fed had merely postponed the inevitable. From Election Day 2004 to April 2008 the dollar lost 20 percent of its value against the euro and 8 percent against the British pound. Use of the Bagehot rules was confirmed by Fed vice chairman Donald Kohn, although he does not seem to understand what the rules are.[56]

Meanwhile, the growth of the Chinese economy accelerated even as the American economy languished in stagflation. Table 5.1 details the changing relations. But these are after revisions. In 2008, the TED said that the American economy was 60 percent larger than that of China in 2004; 40 percent larger in 2005; 29 percent larger in 2006; and only 2 percent larger in 2007. This trend would have suggested that China might surpass the United States in 2008. Then, the Conference Board revised the Chinese historical numbers down historically so that Chinese per capita GDP in the 1970s was lower than that of Cambodia, a country invaded by the United States at the beginning of the decade, Vietnam at the end and in between suffered mass murder and forced deurbanization under Pol Pot. Even with these dubious revisions, the TED showed China's GDP as only 8 percent behind that of the United States. The 2012 release put China ahead by 12 percent under one measure of price parity and 17 percent behind by another measure.

A flood of stories detailed Chinese activity around the globe. At the end of 2004, it was considering investing in Canadian tar sands.[57] In January

TABLE 5.10.
The Fed's Bagehot Maneuver

Month	*Real increase in M3 year-over-year*	*Real interest rate (Prime minus CPI)*
July 2004	1.43	1.25
August	1.64	1.71
September	2.40	1.90
October	2.00	1.53
November	2.20	1.37
December	3.02	1.93
January 2005	3.24	2.25
February	2.90	2.50
March	2.04	2.21
April	1.65	2.25
May	1.96	3.41
June	2.35	3.50
July	1.97	3.05
August	2.61	2.90
September	1.71	2.05
October	2.99	2.55
November	3.77	3.50
December	4.24	3.85
January 2006	3.96	3.27
February	4.45	3.90
	Series Discontinued	

Source: www.federalreserve.gov/datadownload/Choose.aspx?r=H6, accessed June 5, 2012.

2005, the Chinese vice president signed nineteen cooperation agreements with Venezuela. Sinopec agreed to build a $1 billion gas pipeline across Brazil. Negotiations were undertaken with Bolivia, Ecuador, and Peru.[58] In June of 2005, it made a controversial and ultimately unsuccessful bid for the Unocal company. It made a $70 billion commitment to buy Iranian oil and gas.[59] Angola, another oil-rich country, paid the Chinese $2 billion to rebuild its rail system. Nigeria concluded an $8.3 billion railroad deal.[60] In 2002 and 2007, China ordered major increases in its military spending. The size of overall military spending is unclear to analysts given the differing estimates of the Chinese economy. Its official budget at the official exchange rate would be $45 billion, but the CIA estimated it at 4 percent of GDP, which would put it at $400 billion.[61] In 2008, the number of Chinese Internet users surpassed that of the United States.[62] In 1994 Paul

Krugman argued that China, like Japan and the Soviet Union before it, would face diminishing returns because its growth is based on investment and massive mobilization of labor, not productivity gains.[63] This is true, but who knows when that productivity reckoning will occur or what the domestic response will be?

The Return of Russia

The Russian turnaround was also a surprise. As late as 1998, Russia was in de facto default on its international loans.[64] At the end of the Yeltsin regime, the nation stabilized from the post-Soviet tailspin. Russia's industry grew, the government ran a budget surplus, and it repaid international loans. In 1998, Russia had its best showing ever in infant mortality.[65] By 2001, it was up to a share of 2.62 percent of the world economy. The rise in oil prices gave Russia another big boost. On the menu of possibilities outlined in the 1993 book *Russia 2010*, Russia in fact now trends most closely to the model "Double-Headed Eagle" rather than the authors' choice of "Capitalism Russian-style."[66] For Emmanuel Todd, the signal failure of postrevolutionary U.S. foreign policy has been the Russian policy. "Unable to control the real powers of its day . . . America has resorted to making a show of empire by choosing to pursue military and diplomatic actions among a series of puny powers dubbed for dramatic effect 'the axis of evil.'"[67] Todd suggests that American policy was aimed first at promoting further disintegration in the Russian Federation by "stimulating independence movements in the Caucasus and with an American military presence in Central Asia." The second goal was to maintain tension between Russia and the European Union.[68] These attempts failed utterly. Having jettisoned the impoverished central Asian republics, Russia has reestablished ties on its own terms. The invasion of Iraq and the consequent rise of oil prices helped Russia immeasurably. As Russia modernized its oil infrastructure, it passed Saudi Arabia in 2006 to become the largest oil producer in the world.[69] Its exports skyrocketed, and Russia accumulated foreign currency and securities. In August 2006, less than ten years after default, Russia made early payment to complete its loan from the Paris Club of creditor nations.[70] With full freedom of action restored, Russia began to flex its muscles. It made natural gas deals with Uzbekistan and Turkmenistan. It used political pressure to delay the extension of the BTC pipeline to the Kazakh oil fields. It demonstrated it could restrict the flow of gas westward. Finally, in August 2008, Russian forces moved into Georgia and put pressure on the BTC pipeline, the only major gas pipeline in the area that skirts Russian territory.

TABLE 5.11.
Oil Data, 2000–2011 (millions of barrels per day average)

Year	*Global Oil Production*	*Oil and liquids*	*Global Export Pool*	*U.S. Imports*	*China/India Imports*	*Average price per barrel*
2000	68.522	77.768	39.381	9.071	2.737	$27.39
2001	68.117	77.686	38.060	9.328	2.927	$23.00
2002	67.262	76.988	38.041	9.140	3.004	$22.81
2003	69.400	79.593	39.964	9.665	3.594	$27.69
2004	72.446	83.098	43.274	10.088	4.360	$37.66
2005	73.637	84.589	43.361	10.126	4.537	$50.04
2006	73.281	84.675	43.222	10.118	5.061	$58.30
2007	72.800	84.256	42.533	10.031	5.676	$64.20
2008	73.575	85.319	42.136	9.783	6.134	$91.48
2009	72.229	84.336	40.218	9.013	6.880	$53.48
2010	73.948	86.753	40.894	9.213	7.863	$71.21
2011	74.030	87.013	NA	NA	NA	$87.04

Sources: Energy Information Agency, U.S. Department of Energy, accessed June 3, 2012, www.eia.gov/dnav/pet/hist, www.eia.gov/cfapps/ipdbproject, http://inflationdata.com/inflation/inflation_rate/historical_oil_prices_table.

Note: There are considerable disputes over the 2011 data. Compared to the EIA Data, the Texas Railroad Commission states that Texas production was 500,000 barrels a day less, BP says Saudi Arabia produced 500,000 barrels a day less, the U.N.'s Joint Organisations Data Initiative says that Russia produced 600,000 barrels a day less. Inspiration for this table comes from the work of Jeffrey J. Brown, www.graphoilology.blogspot.com.

The Financial Crisis Turns Critical

Political and business fraud and the wars of the 2000s had greatly weakened the American economy and especially its financial system after the exodus of European investment. Growing problems of oil production threatened the global economy. This was an acute problem for the United States because it is so dependent on imported oil. After the price of oil rose in 2000, there was strong incentive to produce more. From 2000 to 2005, as shown in table 5.11, global production rose 9 percent. But since 2005, global oil production has risen only 0.5 percent even as Chinese demand skyrocketed. The American economy came under increasing strain and finally the weakest parts—the housing market and the financial system—broke when the oil price doubled again. The financial markets had never recovered from the aftermath of the election of 2000, and firms had engaged in increasingly reckless behavior sanctioned by the government.

Ultra-low interest rate policies of the Federal Reserve had created a housing bubble. From March 1997 to March 2001, the average federal funds rate set by the Federal Reserve almost matched the market rate of the ten-year

Treasury note. From March 2001 to November 2004, the Fed funds rate was 66 percent lower than the ten-year rate, suggesting that the Fed had diverged sharply from market rates to pump credit into the economy. The housing market was a clear beneficiary even as the economy as a whole hardly grew.[71] Housing prices had traditionally kept pace with incomes and rents. Now an enormous bubble grew. Between 1987 and 2001, the Case-Shiller house price-to-rent ratio fluctuated between 1.0 and 1.2; starting in 2001, it moved up and peaked in the first quarter of 2006 at 1.75; in March 2011 it stood at 1.18. Similarly, the Case-Shiller ratio of price-to-median household income fluctuated between 0.9 and 1.1 before rising above that level in 2001. It peaked at 1.63 in 2006 and stood at 1.06 in May 2011.[72] The rising interest rates hurt homeowners who had financed their mortgage with adjustable interest rates or had expected to refinance with lower interest rates. The Bagehot maneuver to protect the dollar now squeezed growing numbers of people out of their homes. The problem was exacerbated by exploding health care costs and the large numbers of Americans without health insurance. Some people with fully paid houses had taken loans at disadvantageous rates because of illness in their family and then lost their homes.

The crisis of 2008 was concentrated in the larger banks, especially those that did not take advantage of the repeal of the Glass-Steagall Act of 1933 and remained mostly commercially or investment-based. These banks made a growing percentage of their profits from collateralizing debt obligations. A financial institution would bundle loans (most notoriously mortgages) and sell bonds equal to the value of the bundle. In theory, the bundle would contain enough high-quality loans to compensate for any loans that defaulted as long as housing prices kept rising. These bonds could be sold to other institutions or themselves be collateralized in another bundle. The true value of these bundles was thus obscured and a value put on them dictated either by a model that always assumed a rising value of real estate ("mark-to-model") or by established market prices for similar bundles ("mark-to-market"). Like any security, its value is only what someone is willing to pay for it, not any underlying value. There is still no agreement as to the value of these CDOs or how much remains to be written down. In 2009, the Federal Reserve stated that American banks still needed to write down $599 billion, while NYU economist Noriel Roubini put the figure at $1.27 trillion.[73]

In 2007, despite the growing crisis in real estate, all of the major commercial banks reported profits. Some observers doubted these numbers.[74] Washington Mutual, a savings bank, reported a loss, as did all mortgage-based financial institutions and homebuilders.[75] Nevertheless, "WaMu" continued to pay out dividends.[76] In August 2007, the credit market suffered a freeze-up. The Federal Reserve first injected $24 billion in liquidity through open-market operations, then offered $19 billion for mortgage debt. The New York Federal Reserve offered loans that banks could secure with short-term CDOs.[77] But when the analyst Meredith Whitney stated on October 31 that Citigroup was undercapitalized, she was ridiculed and even received death threats.[78] Banks criticized the Goldman, Sachs analyst in November 2007 who predicted a total subprime loss of $200 billion. But by mid-January 2008, the losses were already over $100 billion.[79] Investment bank Bear, Stearns wrote off $2 billion and took its first quarterly loss in eighty-four years, but promised that the remainder of its $44 billion in CDOs were safe.[80]

The brief outline of the 2008 crisis should be familiar. The year opened with Bank of America taking over Countrywide Financial, a company that had been very aggressive in creating mortgages of dubious value. Even in December 2007, Countrywide had been making new subprime loans.[81] BOA thought it was getting a bargain because it was buying Countrywide at one-third of its stated net worth. Some observers suspected that the Fed had brokered this deal after Moody's downgraded many of Countrywide's CDOs.[82] The Fed steadily announced new swap programs with larger amounts and easier terms of collateral. Bear, Stearns failed and was taken over by Chase. The Fed openly brokered this deal and assumed $29 billion in troubled assets.[83] Over the summer, anxiety grew. A list of "zombie banks" circulated on the Internet: today, all of those banks are gone or have been taken over.[84] In July, William Poole, the retired head of the St. Louis Federal Reserve, said that the government-sponsored housing enterprises Freddie Mac and Fannie Mae were insolvent.[85] The turning point, though few realized it, came on July 29, 2008. Merrill Lynch, desperate to raise capital, announced that it was selling "US Super Senior Asset-Backed Security Collateralized Debt Obligations."[86] These had a "gross notional value" of $31 billion, but Merrill had valued them at $11.1 billion, that is, thirty-six cents on the dollar. Their rating was AAA, the highest possible. Merrill sold these bonds to an affiliate of Lone Star Funds for $6.8 billion, that is, 22 cents on the dollar.[87] However, analysts scrutinizing the deal quickly realized that Merrill was sending cash along with the bonds so that the actual value was 5.5 cents on the dollar.[88] This sent shock waves along Wall Street. As long as virtually no bundles were being sold, the banks could cling to the fantasy of "mark to model" and claim them at 80 cents or 60 cents or 36 cents. Now there was a sale made, a real market had been established, and all firms would be compelled to follow the market by accounting rules. Revaluing all the AAA troubled assets at 5.5 cents to the dollar would make most if not all of the major banks insolvent.

September 2008 was the climax. The government put Fannie and Freddie into "conservatorship." The Fed brokered another deal for Bank of America to take over Merrill Lynch and massively expanded its programs. Lehman Brothers filed for bankruptcy. The Fed invoked emergency powers to lend the insurer AIG $85 billion. Chase took WaMu in another brokered deal. Citigroup thought it had acquired Wachovia, but the Fed gave it to Wells Fargo instead. The Treasury Department guaranteed $3.5 trillion in money market deposits.[89] Mitsubishi UFJ bought 21 percent of Morgan Stanley. The credit market almost entirely froze until Congress passed the Troubled Assets Relief Program (TARP) which committed $700 billion to the Treasury Department. The Fed over the next year swapped for $624 billion of mortgage-backed securities at face value while increasing its overall balance by $1.16 trillion.[90] The financial institutions had little interest in selling their troubled assets to the Treasury at what could be deep discounts.

The Treasury therefore used the TARP for other purposes and bought shares of companies. It spent $70 billion buying AIG shares, $50 billion to buy Citigroup shares, and $45 billion to buy Bank of America shares. When Germany nationalized some banks in 1931, it dismissed the boards of directors, installed its own management, and reshaped the banking industry, but the U.S. government did not demand control over policy even though it put the taxpayer on the hook for significant losses. The only bank fully nationalized was the California bank Indy MAC. This bank had been spun off earlier from Countrywide and was so filled with troubled assets that the Federal Deposit Insurance Corporation (FDIC) could not find a buyer and had to administer the bank itself. In this one case, the FDIC launched an innovative program to keep people in their homes and lower the monthly payments.[91]

The shock caused a massive rise in joblessness. As table 5.7 shows, the initial crisis hit the United States far worse than any other country. This put more strain on housing and manufacturing industries. A secondary banking crisis claimed smaller banks in depressed areas and was not related to the shadow banking crisis. While the Obama jobs program put a stop to the free fall, some predict that this is the start of a "long emergency" as the world necessarily moves to a new energy regime.[92] Other countries such as Ireland, Greece, and Spain suffered a second shock and free fall from austerity policies.

As seen from the above tables, the waves from the crisis altered some trends while reinforcing others. While the crisis centered on the United States, many investors still saw American markets as safe havens. The end of the Bush years brought hope that law and order would be restored to American politics and business. The dollar rose steadily after the Lehman Brothers bankruptcy. The TARP and the Obama jobs program required massive borrowing, but there was no problem selling government loans. Both foreign buyers and the Federal Reserve supported the sales strongly, despite a rise in national debt to 100 percent of GDP. The Europeans tended to favor a fall in the euro because it aided their export industries. Germany strengthened its hold in the European Central Bank and gained new highs in employment. Unlike many countries, it suffered no housing crisis. To fight the downturn, most members of Euroland violated the Stability and Growth Pact guidelines. Without the ability to adjust the currency, differentials in bond yields opened. This only became an acute problem in some cases where speculators staged attacks on sovereign debts. The new so-called Treaty on Stability, Coordination, and Governance in the Economic and Monetary Union only makes things worse by calling for a degree of austerity so severe that only one euro member currently meets the guidelines.

Conclusion

From a promising position in the middle of 2000, the United States has fallen into a difficult crisis. The major problems—the high price of energy, the collapse of the credit market, the military quagmire—are both cause and effect of America's loss of position in the world. Europeans fled the American markets after its court overthrew the rule of law. The future indicators of health, education, and nonmilitary research all bode ill for the future. Imperial overstretch and wars across the globe exacerbated the decline of U.S. productivity and competitiveness. American investors and companies moved assets out of their country as the corporate classes showed dwindling interest in American concerns. The crisis that began in 2007 was the culmination of these trends. The crisis created a rush for safe havens that ended the crises of the dollar and U.S. note auctions. This in turn along with the avoidance of austerity spared the United States the problems of Spain and Ireland. The essential problems remain. There is now a strong possibility that the United States will lose the dominance it has enjoyed for 120 years. The United States faces the path walked by Britain after 1900 and the Soviet Union after 1983. Is there any hope for avoiding their fate?

Notes

1. David Rynecki and Andy Serwer, "What's Next?" *Fortune*, October 2, 2000. The actual number was 1148.
2. "The Numbers," *Fortune*, November 13, 2000.

3. Anna Bernasek, "Yes Virginia, There Is a Soft Landing," *Fortune*, December 18, 2000.

4. *New York Times*, November 12, 2001. Despite a misleading headline, the article shows that (depending on the method used) Gore won Florida by between 15 and 46,000 votes. There was no standard that could produce a Bush victory. Gore Vidal, "*Times* Cries Eke! Buries Al Gore," *The Nation*, December 12, 2001, is the classic deconstruction of the *Times* article. Vincent Bugliosi, *The Betrayal of America: How the Supreme Court Undermined the Constitution and Chose Our President* (New York: Thunder's Mouth Press/Nation Books, 2001), and Alan M. Dershowitz, *Supreme Injustice: How the High Court Hijacked Election 2000* (New York: Oxford University Press, 2001), cover the legal absurdities of Bush's lawsuit against Gore.

5. Anna Bernasek, "What Big Profits You Have! But Watch Out—Mighty 2Q Profits Aren't What They Seem," *Fortune*, September 15, 2003.

6. Jesse Drucker, Associated Press, November 28, 2006.

7. Manuel Roig-Franzia, "Credit Crisis Cassandra: Brooksley Born's Unheeded Warning Is a Rueful Echo 10 Years On," *Washington Post*, May 26, 2009.

8. Edmund L. Andrews, "Fed Shrugged as Subprime Crisis Spread," *New York Times*, December 18, 2007; Dennis Hevesi, "Residential Real Estate; Looser U.S. Lending Rules Are Protested," *New York Times*, April 2, 2004.

9. www.treasury.gov/resource-center/data-chart-center/tic/Documents/tressect.txt, accessed June 4, 2012. The data go back to 1978.

10. TIC data for October 2002. s1_glbl.tic, accessed June 4, 2012, www.treasury.gov/resource-center/data-chart-center/tic/Pages/ticarchives.aspx

11. For example from December 2000 to March 2003: Albertson's -60%, Phillip Morris -57%, American Electric Power -70%, American Express -57%, Aquila -86%, Bank of New York -66%, Bristol Myers Squibb -73%, Citigroup -57%, Fleet Financial -60%, General Motors -56%, Lincoln National Bank -53%, May Department Stores -56%, Merck -59%, Merrill Lynch -64%, Morgan Stanley -52%, PNC Bank -57%, Schering-Plough -73%, Sears -69%, Wal-Mart -57%.

12. Floyd Norris, "Strong Gains in U.S., Except by Comparison," *New York Times*, October 13, 2007.

13. "Nominal Major Currencies Dollar Index," accessed June 4, 2012, www.federalreserve.gov/releases/h10/summary/indexn_m.txt.

14. OECD Economic Outlook, May 2006, 22.

15. White House, Office of Management and Budget, Fiscal Year 2009 Budget, "Analytical Perspectives," 241, www.whitehouse.gov/omb/budget/fy2009/pdf/spec.pdf. The FY08 release included the 2002 figure that I have used. The FY13 report, 81–82, states that foreigners have averaged 50 percent of the purchases of U.S. government debt from 2007 to 2011 and now own $4.66 trillion or 46 percent of the public debt. This is the same number I applied in table 5.3 above.

16. "Presentation to the Treasury and the Treasury Borrowing Advisory Committee," 3, accessed June 5, 2012, www.treasury.gov/resource-center/data-chart-center/quarterly-refunding/Documents/mm-2005-q1.pdf. The Treasury Department eliminated the information with the January 2007 release. The Financial Management Service of the Treasury Department lists $8.196 trillion of "marketable debt"

for December 2011. It also lists foreign holdings as $4.996 trillion. This would equal 61 percent, but the figures may not be properly comparable. http://fms.treas.gov/bulletin/index/b2012_3.pdf, accessed June 5, 2012.

17. www.treasurydirect.gov/RI/OFAuctions.

18. OECD Stat Extracts, Health Status, accessed June 3, 2012, http://stats.oecd.org.

19. Paul Krugman, "America Comes Up Short," *New York Times*, June 15, 2007.

20. For example, the International Mathematics and Science Study.

21. Survey of Jon D. Miller et al., *Science*, cited in the *New York Times*, August 11, 2006.

22. *Statistical Abstract 2004*, 163.

23. Stéphane Baldi, George Khalaf, Marianne Perie, and Joel D. Sherman, *International Education Indicators: A Time Series Perspective 1985–1995* (Washington, DC: U.S. Department of Education, Center for Educational Statistics, 2000), 120.

24. Claudia Golden and Lawrence F. Katz, *The Race between Education and Technology* (Cambridge, MA: Harvard University Press, 2008), 330.

25. *Statistical Abstract 2004*, 164.

26. *Statistical Abstract 2004*, 167.

27. Organization for Economic Co-operation and Development (OECD), Education at a Glance 2006 and 2011, tables A1.2a and A1.3a, accessed June 3, 2012, www.oecd.org/edu/highereducationandadultlearning/37363421.xls and www.oecd.org/education/highereducationandadultlearning/48630299.pdf.

28. *New York Times*, September 3, 2006.

29. Lyndsey Layton, "Going Forward: Mass Transit Popularity Surges in U.S.," *Washington Post*, April 30, 2000. American Public Transportation Association press releases of March 12, 2007, www.apta.com/mediacenter/pressreleases/2007/Pages/070312_ten_billion; March 9, 2009, www.apta.com/mediacenter/pressreleases/2009/Pages/090309_ridership; and March 12, 2012, www.apta.com/mediacenter/pressreleases/2012/Pages/120312_2011ridership. All accessed June 5, 2012.

30. U.S. Department of Transportation, "Estimated Miles Driven on All Roads and Streets," accessed June 5, 2012, www.fhwa.dot.gov/policyinformation/travelmonitoring/11novtvt/11novtvt.pdf.

31. Doug Short has compared the DOT data to the American population aged sixteen and over. Doug Short, "Vehicle Miles Driven: Population-Adjusted Sets Another Post-Crisis Low," posted May 21, 2012, accessed June 5, 2012, www.advisorperspectives.com/dshort/updates/DOT-Miles-Driven.php.

32. Jennifer Medina, "In California, Economic Gap of East vs. West," *New York Times*, April 14, 2012.

33. Sam Roberts, "Population Growth in New York City is Outpacing 2010 Census, 2011 Estimates Show," *New York Times*, April 5, 2012.

34. Benjamin Davis and Tony Dutzik, Frontier Group; Phineas Baxandall, U.S. PIRG Education Fund, "Transportation and the New Generation: Why Young People Are Driving Less and What It Means for Transportation Policy," posted April 5, 2012, accessed June 5, 2012, www.frontiergroup.org/reports/fg/transportation-and-new-generation.

35. Jerry Hirsch, "Average Age of Cars on U.S. Roads Rises to Record 10.8 years," *Los Angeles Times*, January 17, 2012.

36. When one compares the U.S. official military budget from 1929 to 2007 to U.S. real economic growth, one finds no significant immediate correlation. Two years out, however, one finds a negative impact of .257, three years out, .288, and four years out, .318. After this, the effect vanishes. Running a regression analysis suggests that for each percentage of GDP devoted to military spending, it takes 23 basis points off real economic growth two years out, 25 points off three years out, and 22 points off four years out. The correlation for this formula is only .100, a weak confirmation. That one can find this over an eighty-year period is suggestive.

37. The U.S. Army/Marine Corps Counterinsurgency Field Manual: U.S. Army field manual 3–24; Marine Corps warfighting publication no. 3-33-5, issued 15 December 2006, 23.

38. *World Almanac 2006*, 72.

39. *Statistical Abstract 2004*, 330.

40. *Statistical Abstract 2004*, 13.

41. Paul Kennedy, *The Rise and Fall of the Great Powers: Economic Change and Military Conflict from 1500 to 2000* (New York: Random House, 1987), 441.

42. *New York Times*, August 15, 2001.

43. *New York Times*, Sunday Business section, October 27, 2002.

44. *New York Times*, December 6, 2002.

45. Liz Alderman and Jack Ewing, "Most Aid to Greece Circles Back," *New York Times*, June 1, 2012.

46. OSCE/ODIHR Election Observation Mission Report, United States of America 2 November 2004 Elections, issued Warsaw 31 March 2005, 7, accessed June 5, 2012, www.osce.org/documents/odihr/elections/usa/14028.

47. OSCE Report, 3.

48. Thomas Crampton, "Observers Find Their Access Limited and the Ballots Complex: Foreign Eyes on US Voting," *International Herald Tribune*, November 4, 2004; "Foreign Voting Observers Feel Like Outsiders," *Los Angeles Times*, October 31, 2004.

49. The CNN screen shots of the 2004 presidential exit poll results on a state-by-state basis were maintained at www.exitpollz.org, but this domain now seems dead. www.truthisall.net/Page10084/page10084 maintains much of the record (posted July 13, 2005, accessed June 5, 2012). Richard Charnin applied detailed mathematical analysis to the election, *Proving Election Fraud: Phantom Voters, Uncounted Votes, and the National Exit Poll* (Bloomington, IN: AuthorHouse, 2010).

50. OSCE Report, 21.

51. OSCE Report, 21.

52. Crampton, "Observers Find Their Access Limited."

53. Minutes of the Federal Reserve's Open Market Committee, December 14, 2004, accessed June 5, 2012, www.federalreserve.gov/formc/minutes/20041214.html.

54. Bagehot, *Lombard Street*, quoted in Clark Johnson, *Gold, France, and the Great Depression, 1919–1932* (New Haven, CT: Yale University Press, 1997), 101–2.

55. Donald L. Kohn, "Comments on 'Interpreting the Unconventional U.S. Monetary Policy of 2007–2009,'" September 10, 2009, accessed June 5, 2012, www.federalreserve.gov/newsevents/speech/kohn20090910a.htm.

56. *New York Times*, December 22, 2004.

57. "China's Oil Diplomacy in Latin America," *New York Times*, March 1, 2005.

58. *New York Times*, June 25, 2005.

59. James Traub, "China's Africa Adventure," *New York Times Magazine*, November 19, 2006, 75–78.

60. *New York Times*, March 5, 2007. This was before the CIA cut its estimate of the Chinese economy by 20 percent.

61. Stefan Halper, *The Beijing Consensus: How the Chinese Authoritarian Model Will Dominate the 21st Century* (New York: Basic Books, 2010), 42.

62. Paul Krugman, "The Myth of Asia's Miracle," *Foreign Affairs*, December 1994, 62–78, quoted in Robert Skidelsky, "The Chinese Shadow," *New York Review of Books*, December 1, 2005, 39.

63. "Oil Wealth Helps Russia in Debt Market," *New York Times*, April 8, 2003.

64. Emmanuel Todd, *After the Empire: The Breakdown of the American Order* (New York: Columbia University Press, 2003), 149–50.

65. Daniel Yergin and Thane Gustavson, *Russia 2010: And What It Means for the World* (New York: Vintage, 1993).

66. Todd, *After the Empire*, 193.

67. Todd, *After the Empire*, 146.

68. U.S. Energy Information Agency, accessed June 5, 2012, www.eia.gov/cfapps/ipdbproject/IEDIndex3.cfm.

69. *New York Times*, June 24, 2006.

70. "Central Asia on Front Line in the Fight for Energy," *New York Times*, December 20, 2007.

71. David Leonhardt, "For Many, a Boom That Wasn't," *New York Times*, April 9, 2008. According to Census Bureau data, the median annual family income in 2000 was $61,000 in constant terms. By 2007, it was $60,500. See also table 5.9. By a different measure, the Federal Reserve stated that median annual family income fell from $49,600 in 2007 to $45,600 in 2010. Binyamin Applbaum, "For U.S. Families, Net Worth Falls to 1990s Levels," *New York Times*, June 12, 2012.

72. "House Prices: Price-to-Rents and Price-to-Median Household Income," *Calculated Risk* (blog), February 22, 2011, accessed June 14, 2012, www.calculatedriskblog.com; "Real Prices and Price-to-Rent," *Calculated Risk* (blog), May 31, 2011, accessed June 14, 2011, www.calculatedriskblog.com.

73. Edmund Andrews, "Troubled Assets Still on Books Could Pose Risk, Panel Says," *New York Times*, August 11, 2009.

74. Floyd Norris, "As Bank Profits Grew, Warning Signs Went Unheeded," *New York Times*, November 16, 2007.

75. "Fortune 500 Ranked within Industries," *Fortune*, May 8, 2008, F-48, F-52, F-57.

76. "WaMu Cuts Dividend, Raises Capital," *Calculated Risk* (blog), December 10, 2007, accessed August 26, 2009, www.calculatedriskblog.com.

77. Greg Ip, "New York Fed Takes Step to Bolster Credit Market," *Wall Street Journal*, August 27, 2007.

78. Steve Rosenbush, "The Analyst Who Rocked Citi," *Business Week*, November 26, 2007.

79. David Gaffen, "Writedowns Surpass $100 billion," January 18, 2008, accessed August 26, 2009, http://blogs.wsj.com/marketbeat/2008/01/18/writedowns-surpass-100-billion.

80. "Bear, Stearns Conference Call," *Calculated Risk* (blog), December 20, 2007, accessed August 26, 2009, www.calculatedriskblog.com.

81. David Mildenberg, "Countrywide Says Foreclosures, Overdue Loans Rise," January 9, 2008, accessed August 26, 2009, www.bloomberg.com/apps/news?id=2060187&sid=qyv.jECplg7w.

82. Herb Greenberg, "Updated: The Real Story on Countrywide," January 10, 2008, accessed August 26, 2009, http://blogs.marketwatch.com/greenberg/2008/01/the-real-story-on-countrywide.

83. "Annex II–Portfolio Overviews," Federal Reserve Bank of New York, accessed June 5, 2012, www.newyorkfed.org/newsevents/speeches/2008/AnnexII.html.

84. The list was Fannie Mae, Freddie Mac, Citigroup, Lehman Brothers, Merrill Lynch, Wachovia, and Washington Mutual. The first three came under government control, Lehman is bankrupt, Merrill under Bank of America, Wachovia under Wells Fargo, and WaMu under Chase.

85. Dawn Kopecki, "Fannie, Freddie 'Insolvent' after Losses, Poole Says," July 11, 2008, www.bloomberg.com/apps/news?pid=20601087&sid=as4DEc5UFopA.

86. Merrill was in a "death spiral" because it had provided "full ratchet" compensation when it raised $12.8 billion from Temesek, the sovereign investment fund of Singapore. If a company subsequently raises money at a lower share price, it must compensate the first creditor by issuing new shares. This tends to depress share prices, leading to a further issuance. Michael Shedlock, "Death Spiral Financing at WaMu and Merrill," July 23, 2008, accessed September 5, 2009, http://globaleconomicanalysis.blogspot.com/2008/07/death-spiral-financing-at-wamu-and-merrill.html.

87. Merrill Lynch Press Release, July 29, 2008, accessed August 25, 2009, www.ml.com/index.asp?id=7695_7696_8149_88278_101366_103431.

88. John Glover, "Merrill Gives Up Gains, Is 'On Hook for CDO Losses,'" Bloomberg News, July 30, 2008, accessed September 5, 2009, www.bloomberg.com/apps/news?pid=20601087&sid=aQRdW281niUw&refer=home. Louise Story, "A Deal at Merrill Puts Spotlight on Others," *New York Times*, July 30, 2008.

89. Joe Nocera, "The Risk in Money Funds," *New York Times*, August 29, 2009.

90. Report of August 27, 2009, U.S. Federal Reserve, accessed August 30, 2009, www.federalreserve.gov/datadownload/Choose.aspx?rel=H41.

91. Michael M. Phillips and Ruth Simon, "FDIC Plan Tests Limits of Leniency," *Wall Street Journal*, November 1, 2008.

92. Notably James Howard Kunstler, *The Long Emergency: Surviving the End of Oil, Climate Change, and Other Converging Catastrophes of the Twenty-First Century* (New York: Grove Press, 2005).

Conclusion: After U.S. Dominance

This study set out to examine quantitative methods of measuring power through history. Dominance was defined as the relation of the leading power to the second-largest power of the day. Hegemony was defined as the relation of the leading power to the next three combined. Gross domestic product was the main measurement used to derive these numbers, although I immediately noted its limitations. Hegemony in modern times is rarer than many thought. By the numbers, China enjoyed a hegemony for centuries, but its low per capita GDP, its lack of domestic market because of income inequality, and its unwillingness to travel very far made this fact largely irrelevant except for its neighborhood of East Asia. In Europe, there was no hegemony except perhaps during the height of the Napoleonic Empire. The period of British dominance in Europe did not last eighty years, and Britain confined itself to limited actions and easy opponents. When it became more adventurous after Palmerston's death in 1865, it got into trouble and lost its dominance.

The United States rose to hegemony from the 1820s. Relative to the rest of the world, the United States was wealthier by some measures in 1820 than it was in 2008. Its relative life expectancy was better in 1820 than in 2008. The United States expanded its resource base from 1820 to 1870 while maintaining its wealth position. Although obstructionists retarded development, the breakthroughs in transportation and education that came after the Civil War put the United States on the road to dominance. Industrialization and immigration-swelled population growth allowed the United States to claim the top position in the world at the end of the 1880s. Internal problems consumed Russia and Britain and they were not able to claim dominance. American economic growth was plowed back into public health, education, and transportation to plant the seeds for future growth. After World War I devastated Europe, the United States moved to a position of hegemony. After sixty years of spectacular growth, a setback was inevitable. The Great Depression was caused in part by global conditions and in part by American self-inflicted wounds. While many died in the Dust Bowl, the Depression was not severe enough to destroy the economic base. The Texas oil fields developed and formed the foundation for the next forty years of economic growth. World War II showed the full potential of the American economy. By the beginning of the 1950s, American hegemony was greater than ever.

But the diversion of resources to maintain an American empire gradually accomplished what the Depression could not. Education, health, and transport slowly declined relative to the rest of the world. The loss of the Vietnam War and the energy crisis were terrible shocks, but these only led to a greater determination to hold and expand the empire. Scholars regularly sounded alarms, and politicians regularly announced reforms, but conditions only grew worse. Only during the 1990s was there a concerted attempt to repair the damage, but that decade ended with the greatest calamity yet. American influence has been in free fall since the end of 2000. The unprecedented problems of 2008 were the culmination of events of the previous fifty years. The interrelated problems of energy, health care, and housing cost millions their jobs and the homes of their dreams. This is perhaps the beginning of what James Howard Kunstler termed "the long emergency" when all previous policies and assumptions will be abandoned.

We may identify this first as a crisis of hegemony. Paul Kennedy in *The Rise and Fall of the Great Powers* described a recurrent pattern: a power such as Habsburg Spain or Britain rises, becomes arrogant in its power, and falls into imperial overstretch. The nation devotes so many resources to military adventures that there are not enough to support the economic base. When that base crumbles, the resources for the military evaporate, and the reign of the great power has ended. This study has posited that health, education, and transportation are keys to higher productivity (reflected in per capita GDP). A more efficient exploitation of resources creates higher GDP and thus military power. In 1987, Kennedy identified the beginning of a hegemony crisis for the United States. The decline since 2000 has been breathtaking and few around the world seem able to adjust to the new reality.

After 2005, a second type of crisis cut across and interacted with the crisis of hegemony. This is a crisis of energy and finance. Energy has driven the unprecedented growth that sets the modern economy apart from the ancient and medieval economies. England was aided by its ability to support 67 percent more horsepower than France, peat-burning powered development in the Netherlands, then came the change from wood-burning to coal burning that was a basic shift of the Industrial Revolution.[1] The combination of oil and the internal-combustion engine that appeared in the twentieth century was even more intensive. The American ability to export unlimited amounts of oil was a key to victory in World War II. Had the Japanese destroyed the fuel tanks at Pearl Harbor and left the ships alone, they would have dealt a far more crippling blow. The United States was a net exporter of oil until 1948 and then the world's leading producer.[2] The shift in the balance of global oil production helped lead to the multipolar world that developed by the 1970s. Then came the first shock wave to hit the U.S. economy. U.S. oil production hit an all-time peak of production at 9.77 million barrels a day in 1970 and even the advent of production in Alaska could not restore that peak. Production stayed on a bumpy plateau for about seventeen years, and then had a sharp fall to about 60 percent of the peak. Not coincidentally, 1970 also marks the peak in American real wages and individual median income. Household income has only risen modestly because of second incomes as reflected in the participation rates.

The price of oil rose after 1999 and there was strong incentive to produce more. From 2001 to 2005, global production rose 8 percent as one would expect with rising prices and increasing incentive to bring marginal sources of oil on line. In 2005, global oil production rose 1.6 percent as Chinese demand skyrocketed. Then the system broke as oil production peaked. This was more serious because the largest exporters such as Saudi Arabia and Russia needed more oil for their own needs. The pool of exportable oil and oil-like liquids contracted. To continue trend growth required oil production and export growth that simply did not happen. Finally, the Chinese were able to use their enormous trade surplus accounts to buy up all the oil they needed, leaving other nations short. To a lesser degree India also used its current account surpluses. By 2010, the export oil market had shrunk while the share taken by China and India had risen from 10.5 percent to 19 percent. Oil is vital to the American economy because petroleum is the biggest single contributor of energy with almost 40 percent of the total. Most of that is used in transportation.[3]

Geologist Jeffrey Brown has been the main proponent of the "export land model." He has noted that nations as different as the United Kingdom and Indonesia had to cease net exports of oil six to eight years after their production peaked. Brown suggests that the pool of exported oil may fall to 13 million barrels a day by 2018. Half of the American oil supply and one-fifth of the entire American energy demand comes from imported oil.[4] The plateau halted economic growth except in those countries that had sufficient cash on hand to pay any price for oil. "Demand destruction" occurred as many people and businesses could not afford high prices. It is likely to affect the poor and the poor nations most. There are probably interior areas of Africa and Asia that have reverted to a premodern transportation system. If the U.S. peak of 1970 constituted the first shock wave, the second was the world production peak of 2006 and the move to a bumpy plateau. The American economy came under increasing strain and the weakest parts—the housing market and the financial system—broke when the oil price doubled again. By 2011, U.S. oil consumption had fallen back to its 1973 level.[5]

There has been a concerted attempt to assure the public that all is right or could be right with oil. These articles are deeply misleading either by conflation, omission, or outright errors. It is true that when the cost of oil approached $100 a barrel, new sources became economical, such as the tar sands in Canada. Since 2009, the number of oil rigs in the United States has increased sevenfold. Many of these use hydraulic fracturing and horizontal drilling to extract "tight oil." These techniques are not new as the media suggest. They were developed thirty-five years ago. Only now have tight-oil formations such as the Baaken Shale in North Dakota become economical to drill. The U.S. Energy Department states that this 610 percent rig growth has generated a 19 percent growth in U.S. oil production.[6] Despite this enormous investment and incentive, it has barely balanced the decline in other sources.

Conflation is the mixing of high-energy crude oil with lesser liquids such as natural gas condensate and ethanol. These other forms contain less energy by volume and require more energy to be invested so that they have a lower Energy Return on (Energy) Invested (EROI or EROEI) ratio. Ethanol by one measure yields only 7 percent more energy than the energy invested.[7] Compare this to the estimates of the oil drilling before 1972 where the yield was 1900%.[8] Ethanol production has increased enormously and in measures of "all liquids" gets counted as equal to oil. Since 2000, the United States has increased by sevenfold its production of ethanol fuel.[9] This production has now reached diminishing returns. Not only did the price of corn rise to a level not seen for decades, but the demand for wheat caused its price to double, and the price of beef rose by 50 percent. Some of the leading importers of grain are poor nations. Egypt is the leading importer of wheat in the world by a large margin and is the fourth-ranked global importer of corn.[10] Food issues drove much of the unrest there. To avoid riots, governments heavily subsidize food prices, which leads to other economic problems. We will not see another rapid increase in ethanol fuel production.

There is a conflation of all fossil fuels, mixing the liquids with natural gas and coal. There are several problems. Not only do these sources have different energy content, but coal's energy content varies wildly from anthracite to lignite. If anyone has estimated that total remaining energy content of American coal, it remains a secret. The average quality of coal mined has declined for many years. As quality gets lower, coal mining becomes more costly and damaging to the environment. There is only one synfuels plant left in the United States, located in North Dakota, that could convert coal to oil. A shift to transportation run on natural gas would require a new fueling infrastructure and a new vehicle fleet. The slow move to electric and hybrid cars and the apparently indestructible appeal of the pickup truck show that a transformation of the personal vehicle is unlikely.

Gullibility is shown by reference to growing global oil reserves. Most of these are due to three nations: Iraq, Iran, and Saudi Arabia. None have been audited. Iraq and Iran have played a game of leap frog for decades. One announces it has more reserves, the other revises its figure to jump ahead, then the other adjusts its reserves. There is little evidence that these reserves are real. Saudi Arabia has announced regularly that despite pumping more than three billion barrels of oil a year for many years, its reserves have not fallen a bit. Year after year, they magically refill. By the estimate of Sam Foucher, assuming that the Saudi ultimate recoverable reserve is 224 billion barrels, Saudi Arabia will stop exporting oil around 2040.[11] That will likely mark the effective end of the export market and will be the third oil shock wave.

Finally, there is outright error. Statements are thrown around such as the United States alone has a hundred years of oil supplies. This assertion assumes that kerogen, common in the Rocky Mountains, is oil. It is not. It is an oil precursor. It must be mined like coal, then crushed and heated at about 650 degrees Fahrenheit for two to three years in place.[12] In the 1970s, oil companies explored kerogen exploitation. They found that not only is production too expensive but it consumes more energy than is yielded. In other words, its EROEI is under one. May 2, 1982, is still remembered in northwest Colorado as "Black Sunday" when Exxon announced it was abandoning its kerogen project. Kerogen has less energy density than dried cow dung.[13]

A similar error is the transformation of "net oil product exporter" to "net oil exporter." The United States remains a net oil importer. The collapse of domestic demand for gasoline and other products has led refineries to import oil to keep operating and then to ship the products abroad. This will not last for very long. Conoco and Sunoco are closing three refineries in the Philadelphia area and others will follow as there is no need for them and profit margins are low.[14] It is becoming clear that cheap oil will never return.

What is the real value of oil? A barrel contains the energy equivalent of 8,000 people working for an hour. Minimum wage pay for these workers would equal $58,000.[15] At $100 a barrel, oil is cheap. A cup of gasoline costs less than a cup of coffee at McDonald's. Here is a paradox: we think of oil as expensive but it is cheap relative to its real value. U.S. gas prices might go to $10 a gallon but people will figure out ways to cope. When I was in Cairo, I was astonished by the traffic and the ways people lived with expensive gas: hold onto cars for forty years, turn many vehicles into improvised taxis stuffed with as much humanity as physically possible, invent six lanes on a four-lane highway, have the government subsidize cheaper fuel. The cars and roads will not disappear. Everything will just get a little shabbier. Oil is indispensable because of its abundance, its concentrated energy, and its versatility. Other energy sources are poor substitutes. Hardship, for the moment, will be seen in the marginal and impoverished areas of the world.

The biggest impact of oil is on the credit supply, if I may be allowed to venture into the theoretical. Critics often claim that credit is built on nothing or even that we should move to a credit-free society. Credit built this modern economic world. Energy gives value to the credit. The peat of the Netherlands, the coal of England and Wales, and then oil allowed for the massive expansion of the world economy. When that $58,000 barrel of oil is consumed, that value is not entirely destroyed. At least part of the value lives on in the value of what it was burned for, but also I suspect a surplus commodity value that can be drawn upon as credit. The enormous and excessive volume of credit in World War I and the 1920s coincided with marriage of oil and the internal combustion engine. Not by chance. The world left the gold standard after 1930 when it was too confining to economic growth. It substituted an oil standard, even if treaties did not fix values as the gold standard treaties did. For eighty years, the growth in oil production allowed for stupendous growth in credit and unprecedented economic and population growth.

The oil and financial crisis that started in 2007 helped the United States in some ways. As seen in chapter 5, it was having difficulty selling its longer-term debt on the market. The flight to safety since 2008 has boosted the dollar and provided plenty of buyers for U.S. Treasury securities. The crisis led the European Union to inflict a series of wounds upon itself. Mortgaging a country to pay off the stockholders and bondholders of a bank is a recipe for disaster. Compounding that with austerity is a recipe for revolution. The crisis did not slow down the rise of China, which used its surplus reserves to outbid others for oil. As the U.S. economy stagnated after 2006, the Chinese caught up.

It seems likely that China will soon fall back. Rapid economic expansion brings a host of social and economic problems that a nation must accommodate. China's crony capitalism, environmental degradation, economic controls, local overdevelopment, and political opacity are all dangerous conditions. Its very success can contain the seeds of recession. As oil grows more expensive, the American consumer cannot buy as many goods from China. Many of these goods are discretionary. As the price of oil rises, so do transportation costs. These trends have already led to a modest revival of American manufacturing. The Chinese trade surplus has diminished and in some months disappeared entirely. This in turn means that China has a lower cash reserve to buy oil. This puts downward pressure on the price of oil, creating more American desire to buy Chinese discretionary goods, increasing the Chinese trade surplus, and allowing them to bid up the price of oil. We have already gone through one or two of these cycles and may go through more. As in the 1930s, globalization is receding.

In modern world history, there has only been one passing of dominance before: from China to the United States in the 1880s. This marked the culmination of a century of crisis for China. However, there were no major international wars marking this event unless one counts the Sino-Japanese War of 1894–1895. Modern European history, however, is rather different. The passing of dominance from France to Britain was marked by the wars of the French Revolution and Napoleon. The loss of dominance by Britain to Germany prefaced World War I. Without ignoring personal agency and immediate circumstances, it is possible to see the two world wars and the watchful peace that followed as a long struggle among Britain, Russia, and Germany with Germany finally emerging as the victor. As A. J. P. Taylor pointed out long ago, the Germans' position would have been immeasurably better without the wars.

There is nothing intrinsically wrong with losing dominance. One may settle back and enjoy wealth and prosperity. There is always a place for national defense, but it should be for no more than that, defense. When the United States lost hegemony in the early 1970s, it was marked by an inability to defeat a poor population of 42 million. With Iraq, the United States has not been able to defeat a population of 25 million. Should the United States truly wish to pursue empire, it can still overwhelm tiny, impoverished populations in the Americas of 10 million or less. It can still dominate the Caribbean and Central America, if it chooses to. It could probably even conquer Venezuela which has a population of about the same size as Iraq but is less distant. The Germans emerged triumphant at the close of the century, but despite the wars, not because of them. Just because the passing of dominance in Europe was marked in blood, this does not have to be a political law. There is no natural source of conflict between China and the United States. Britain and Russia cooperated grudgingly in two world wars. China and the United States can cooperate grudgingly in dealing with global crises of this century.

But the time has come to ask whether any of this is worth it. No nation can conquer the United States. No nation can economically or militarily overawe the United States. The only danger along these lines would be if the United States split into a number of republics as the Soviet Union did at the end of 1991. This would leave imbalances in population, financial wealth, and mineral wealth because the sum of the parts is less than the whole. The breakup of the Austro-Hungarian Empire in 1918 serves as a better analogy than the Soviet example, which left the huge Russian heartland undivided. This breakup can only happen (1) at the end of a cataclysmic war where the United States was on the losing side and the victors decided to occupy and break up the United States or (2) if large segments of the American people felt that they are no longer represented and rewarded by being part of a united country. This would not be the secession of the obstructionist confederacy that brought about the result it feared most, but rather a secession of the wealthier, better-educated part seeing its resources wasted on wars and corruption as its children face a life of reduced prosperity.

Even without the current tensions, demographics and previous policies would dictate a time of growing tension until the 2030s. This does not even account for important issues of environmental degradation and climate change whose effects we barely understand. It could be that the explosion in autism and allergies is due to chemical pollution and trillions of dollars would have to be used for cleanup. It could be that global heating will marginalize some farmland from North Dakota to Texas and shift the entire American food supply system.

Since the long emergency began much of the world has rationed gasoline and electricity, not by government order, but by price. Oil use in the United States has fallen by 10 percent, mostly in transportation. The percentage of the American population holding a job is barely above the level of 1969, and real wages are stuck at the 1970 level. What recovery there has been has been concentrated overwhelmingly in the richer classes. Millions have been pushed out of the labor force. No wonder so many people are angry.

In conclusion, money and credit still exist for the United States. Japan's national debt as a ratio of the economy is twice that of the United States, and its interest rates are low. That suggests that the United States could fund a dozen programs of the size of the 2009 Obama jobs act. One needs to focus spending on making a fair and orderly transition to a new energy regime using less oil more efficiently. A peacetime military budget would correct debt and trade problems. There must be focus on increasing productivity by modernizing transportation, improving education, and bringing American health care results to the level of other developed nations. Increased productivity can compensate for a stagnating energy supply to provide a measure of growth. Complacency is the biggest enemy. Twilight's gleam can long endure.

Notes

1. Tracy Dennison and James Simpson, "Agriculture," in *The Cambridge Economic History of Modern Europe*, vol. 1, *1700 to 1870*, eds. Stephen Broadberry and Kevin O' Rourke (New York: Cambridge University Press, 2010), 155; Jan de Vries and Ael van der Woude, *The First Modern Economy: Success, Failure, and Perseverance of the Dutch Economy, 1500–1815* (New York: Cambridge University Press, 1997), 711.

2. Irvine H. Anderson, *ARAMCO, The United States and Saudi Arabia* (Princeton, NJ: Princeton University Press, 1981), 35–81.

3. U.S. Department of Energy, Energy Information Administration, Monthly Energy Review, May 2012, "Primary Energy Consumption by Source," accessed June 7, 2012, www.eia.gov/totalenergy/data/monthly/pdf/sect1_7.pdf.

4. Jeffrey J. Brown and Sam Foucher, "Declining Net Oil Exports—a Temporary Decline or Long-Term Trend?," *GraphOilogy* (blog), posted September 25, 2007, accessed August 22, 2010, www.graphoilogy.blogspot.com.

5. U.S. Department of Energy, "Primary Energy Consumption by Source."

6. www.eia.gov/dnav/ng/hist/ertrro_xr0_nus_cm.htm, released June 4, 2012, accessed June 7, 2012.

7. David Murphy, "New Perspectives on the Energy Return on (Energy) Investment of Corn Ethanol," *Environment, Development, and Sustainability* 13, no. 1:179–202.

8. Megan C. Guilford, Charles A.S. Hall, Pete O'Connor, and Cutler J. Cleveland, "A New Long Term Assessment of Energy Return on Investment (EROI) for U.S. Oil and Gas Discovery and Production," *Sustainability* 3 (2001): 1866–87.

9. "Maps and Data," Alternative Fuels Data Center, U.S. Department of Energy, accessed June 7, 2012, www.afdc.energy.gov/afdc/data.

10. Food and Agriculture Organization of the United Nations, Agribusiness Handbook, 18.

11. Jeffrey J. Brown and Sam Foucher, "A Quantitative Assessment of Future Net Oil Exports by the Top Five Net Oil Exporters," *GraphOilogy* (blog), posted January 7, 2008, accessed June 6, 2012, www.graphoilogy.blogspot.com.

12. http://lostscis.anl.gov/guide/oilshale, accessed June 7, 2012.

13. Dung has an energy density of 15.5 megajoules per kilogram according to "Energy Density," *Wikipedia*, accessed June 7, 2012, http://en.wikipedia.org/wiki. http://fossil.energy.gov/programs/resources/npr/Oil_Shale_Reserve_Fact_Sheet states the richest oil shales yield sixty gallons of oil per ton, which translates to 11.6 megajoules per kilogram.

14. Mathew Philips, "East Coast Gas Squeeze Expected," *Bloomberg Businessweek*, March 1, 2012.

15. Luis de Sousa, "What Is a Human Being Worth (in Terms of Energy)?," *The Oil Drum: Europe*, posted July 20, 2008, accessed June 7, 2012, http://europe.theoildrum.com/node/4315.

Selected Bibliography

Reference Material

The Conference Board Total Economy Database. www.conference-board.org/data/economydatabase.

Correlates of War Project, Pennsylvania State University. Last modified June 2010. www.correlatesofwar.org.

Maddison, Angus. *Chinese Economic Performance in the Long Run.* Paris: OECD, 1998.

———. *The World Economy: A Millennial Perspective.* Paris: OECD, 2001.

Mitchell, Brian. *European Historical Statistics.* Abridged ed. New York: Columbia University Press, 1978.

———. *International Historical Statistics: Africa, Asia, and Oceania.* New York: Stockton Press, 1995.

——— . *International Historical Statistics, 1750–2005: The Americas.* New York: Palgrave Macmillan, 2008.

Steckel, Richard H. "A History of the Standard of Living in the United States." Last modified February 1, 2010. http://eh.net/encyclopedia/article/steckel.standard.living.us.

United States Central Intelligence Agency. *World Factbook.* Various years.

United States Department of Commerce. *Statistical Abstract of the United States.* Various years.

U.S. White House, Office of Management and Budget. The Budget for the Fiscal Year, Historical Tables, Analytical Perspectives. Various years.

World Almanac. Various years.

Primary Sources

OSCE/ODIHR Election Observation Mission Report. United States of America 2 November 2004 Elections. Issued Warsaw 31 March 2005.

Secondary Sources

Anderson, Jack, with James Boyd. *Fiasco.* New York: Times Books, 1983.

Bacevich, Andrew, *American Empire: The Realities and Consequences of U.S. Diplomacy.* Cambridge, MA: Harvard University Press, 2002.

Bairoch, Paul. "International Industrialization Levels from 1750 to 1980." *Journal of European Economic History,* Fall 1982, 296–304.

Braudel, Fernand. *Civilization and Capitalism 15th–18th Century.* Vol. 2, *The Wheels of Commerce.* New York: Harper and Row, 1982.

Brenner, Robert. *The Boom and the Bubble: The U.S. in the World Economy.* London: Verso, 2002.

Brown, Judith, and Wm. Roger Louis, eds. *The Oxford History of the British Empire: The Twentieth Century.* New York: Oxford University Press, 1999.

Cameron, Rondo. *A Concise Economic History of the World: From Paleolithic Times to the Present.* 2nd ed. New York: Oxford University Press, 1992.

Clingingsmith, David, and Jeffrey G. Williamson. "Deindustrialization in 18th and 19th Century India: Mughal Decline, Climate Shocks and British Industrial Ascent." *Explorations in Economic History* 45, no. 3 (2008).

Cockburn, Andrew. *The Threat: Inside the Soviet Military Machine.* New York: Vintage Books, 1984.

Findlay, Ronald, and Kevin O'Rourke. *Power and Plenty: Trade, War, and the World Economy in the Second Millennium.* Princeton, NJ: Princeton University Press, 2007.

Friedberg, Aaron L. *A Contest for Supremacy: China, America and the Struggle for Mastery in Asia.* New York: Norton, 2011.

———. *The Weary Titan: Britain and the Experience of Relative Decline, 1895–1905.* Princeton, NJ: Princeton University Press, 1988.

Gash, Norman. *Aristocracy and People: Britain, 1815–1865.* Cambridge, MA: Harvard University Press, 1979.

Golden, Claudia, and Lawrence F. Katz. *The Race between Education and Technology.* Cambridge, MA: Harvard University Press, 2008.

Halper, Stefan. *The Beijing Consensus: How the Chinese Authoritarian Model Will Dominate the 21st Century.* New York: Basic Books, 2010.

Harrison, Mark, ed. *The Economics of World War II: Six Great Powers in International Comparison.* New York: Cambridge University Press, 1998.

Hobsbawm, Eric J. *The Pelican Economic History of Britain.* Vol. 3, *Industry and Empire.* New York: Penguin, 1968.

Hoppen, K. Theodore. *The Mid-Victorian Generation, 1846–1886.* New York: Oxford University Press, 1998.

Hoppit, Julian. *A Land of Liberty? England 1689–1727.* New York: Oxford University Press, 2000.

Jacques, Martin. *When China Rules the World: The End of the Western World and the Birth of a New Global Order.* New York: Penguin, 2009.

Johnson, Chalmers. *The Sorrows of Empire: Militarism, Secrecy, and the End of the Republic.* New York: Owl Books, 2004.

Kagan, Robert. *The World America Made.* New York: Knopf, 2012.

Kennedy, Paul. *The Rise and Fall of the Great Powers: Economic Change and Military Conflict from 1500 to 2000.* New York: Random House, 1987.

Kindleberger, Charles P. *A Financial History of Western Europe.* 2nd ed. Oxford: Oxford University Press, 1993.

Kunstler, James Howard. *The Long Emergency: Surviving the End of Oil, Climate Change, and Other Converging Catastrophes of the Twenty-First Century.* New York: Grove Press, 2005.

Kupchan, Charles. *The End of the American Era: U.S. Foreign Policy and the Geopolitics of the Twenty-First Century.* New York: Vintage, 2002.

Landes, David. *The Wealth and Poverty of Nations: Why Some Are So Rich and Some So Poor.* New York: Norton, 1998.

Marshall, P. J., ed. *The Oxford History of the British Empire: The Eighteenth Century.* New York: Oxford University Press, 1998.

O'Rourke, Kevin, and Jeffrey G. Williamson. *Globalization and History: The Evolution of a Nineteenth-Century Atlantic Economy.* Cambridge, MA: Harvard University Press, 1999.

———. "When Did Globalization Begin?" *European Review of Economic History* 6 (2002): 23–50.

Porter, Andrew, ed. *The Oxford History of the British Empire: The Nineteenth Century.* New York: Oxford University Press, 1999.

Riley, James C. *Rising Life Expectancy: A Global History.* New York: Cambridge University Press, 2001.

Roy, Tirthanker. "Economic History and Modern India: Refining the Link." *Journal of Economic Perspectives* 16:109–30.

Searle, G. R. *A New England? Peace and War 1886–1918.* New York: Oxford University Press, 2004.

Todd, Emmanuel. *After the Empire: The Breakdown of the American Order.* New York: Columbia University Press, 2003.

Wong, R. Bin. *China Transformed: Historical Change and the Limits of European Expansion.* Ithaca, NY: Cornell University Press, 1997.

Index

About the Author

Edmund Clingan was educated at the City University of New York and the University of Bonn. He received his MA and PhD in history from the University of Wisconsin–Madison. His books include *Finance from Kaiser to Führer: Budget Politics in Germany, 1912–1934* and *The Lives of Hans Luther, 1879–1962: German Chancellor, Reichsbank President, and Hitler's Ambassador.* He is currently associate professor of history at Queensborough Community College, City University of New York.

www.ingramcontent.com/pod-product-compliance
Lightning Source LLC
Chambersburg PA
CBHW051251200926
51612CB00001B/7
9780739171158